Elk
River

Genoa

Nine Mile Point

Robert E.
Ginna

Yankee

Indian
Point

Dresden

Peach
Bottom

Carolinas-Virginia

"**Revolution** is based on **land. Land** is the basis of all independence. Land is the basis of **freedom, justice** and **equality**"

—Malcolm X

"**Message to the grassroots,**"
November 10, 1963

Urban Wilds

gardeners' stories of the struggle for land and justice

edited by cleo woelfle-erskine

to Gerald Hairston, guiding spirit of the Detroit Agriculture Network

water/under/ground publications   a pollinators exchange
2nd edition, fall 2002

Urban Wilds: gardeners' stories of the struggle for land and justice • edited by cleo woelfle-erskine
2nd edition copyright © 2003, not-for-profit distribution of unedited articles encouraged
rights held by individual authors and artists
ISBN: 0-9727072-0-4

design by Greg Jalbert and cleo • title by Brian • cover collage by Sarah Lyzyrd • tree drawing by Annie Danger

"Swaling a Parking Lot" by Dan Dorsey first appeared in the Permaculture Drylands Journal
"Guerrilla Solar" by Laura Allen first appeared in Home Power magazine
"Seeds in the City" by Andrea del Moral first appeared in "food not lawns: cultivating a moral landscape"

printing of first edition made possible by donations from the Fund for Wild Nature, Bruce Triggs and Peter Erskine
printed at Inkworks Press on recycled paper using soy based ink

A portion of proceeds from the sale of this book support the work of these gardeners and organizations. In addition, a 25-cent "tree tax" is included in the cover price, and is sent directly to organizations working in sustainable forestry.

water/under/ground publications
P.O. Box 3831
Oakland, CA 94609
www.urbanwilds.org

distributed by:
AK Press
674-A 23rd St.Oakland, CA 94612-1163
(510) 208-1700
www.akpress.com

Individual copies and sales to the trades through AK Press.

Nonprofit organizations or distributors please contact water/under/ground for bulk ordering information.

Under pavement. Under a shimmering crust of broken glass and weeds, the dark earth endures. We are dispossessed of our most basic human right—to cultivate the land. But in cities across North America, people are taking back this right and resisting corporate control of food and livelihood. Here are some of their stories.

photo by jeff conant

mural, South Bronx, NY

This book was written by gardeners for the revolutionaries who don't have good food to eat, for the gardeners who spend long afternoons in the garden telling stories, the elders who hold volumes of agricultural knowledge and the young ones watching their first season's garden grow. These stories are meant as a starting point, a few guideposts on a journey that follows many paths.

This project is a collaboration between many people: the gardeners who shared their stories and food and brought their struggles to life; the contributors who translate these movements for the world at large. The artists and photographers: Sarah Lyzyrd, Annie Danger, Lucha, Jeff Conant, Aresh Javadi, Rubisel, Greg Jalbert, Loren Hellfire, Tiffany and Eric Drooker. Special thanks to Daniel and for editing early versions of the interviews and seeing the project through to the end, and to Andrea, partner in crime, for hitching misadventures past and future. Lana, Mark, Blake, Gretchen and Peter (and anyone else I could pin down) also did tons of editing on a ridiculously short schedule. Thanks to Sascha and all the free voicemail companies for keeping

me going at phone booths on many a lonely road and to Lisa Camisa for turning me on to Not For Rent which inspired the format of this book. Spring came up with the "Urban Wilds" title and found both funding and a printer for the first edition. The Fund for Wild Nature, Bruce Triggs and Peter Erskine provided the funds to print the guide. Greg Jalbert provided hours of layout assistance as well as dozens of "whimsical" drawings. No thanks to the Voice of Reason, which would have had me lying on the beach instead of putting out this book again. All writing, drawings and photos by cleo unless credited otherwise.

A shoutout to the Guerrilla Graywater Girls, the Pollinators past, present and future, to the youth of the Bay Area who care about our world, and to everyone else who's helped this book come alive.

For everything else, Joel, Devon, Mary, Ea, Blake and Mike, my touchstones.

cleo, Oakland, CA December 26, 200

vii

Contents

Introduction: The Church of Everlasting Freeway Noise

My window in Oakland, California looks out on a five-lane freeway offramp; the f eeway itself is sunken, but the rhythmic roar rises and falls, mixed in with sirens, and sometimes the sound of the rain. The nearest open space, ten blocks to the south, is a strip of grass around a man-made lake, the remnant of a large estuary system. The insects that live in the sterile lawn around the lake are an important source of food for Canada Geese. You see the geese in the strip of green dodging joggers in the evening.

The rest of the estuary is constricted by the marina, the freeway, railroad bridges and new "live-work" development. The closest place to get down to the bay is three miles away, though the water itself is only five blocks from my house, beyond an impenetrable wall of ship-yards and the abandoned naval station.

When I moved to this city two and a half years ago, I lived in a large house with a bunch of people to keep the rent down. On the corner was Easy Liquors #2. There was a vacant lot next door to the vacant fried chicken place that opened up for a few months as an all-night juke joint. People had dug up an engine block, broken glass and needles and planted some tomatoes and arugula in our backyard. I sheet mulched the weeds, planted some herbs and wild greens, and for one summer grew a crop of beans and some collard greens.

"You could feel a huge rush of energy come surging out of the ground when they bulldozed Esperanza garden. All the years of work and play and laughter, all the care and children's voices, all the planning and struggle and people who were a part of the garden flew up into the sky and scattered, like seeds of hope. Some of those seeds got planted in D.C. last week. Maybe some took root in your life. The garden was destroyed, but the land remains."

After starting and leaving many gardens at rented or squatted houses, I wasn't sure about putting so much work into a house we didn't even have a lease on. But the people who ran the juke joint admired our collard greens and cooked them up once in a while. Our neighbors came over to get lemons for lemonade. People brought tricks to our garden, smoked crack there, and slept in the back sometimes, but they never messed with the plants. Some nights we would roast corn and potatoes in the firepit and you could hear the music rippling out into the darkness.

Within three months, three garden projects with five-year histories were evicted. First our slumhouse by the freeway was sold for $250,000. Next, a community garden bordering one of the few creeks in the east bay that runs outside of a culvert was evicted to be turned into a parking lot. A month later, a 3/4 acre community urban farm next to a $50 million test plot of genetically engineered corn was evicted by the University of California. The hand-dug beds that had been carefully mulched and amended for five years were plowed under, and to this day remain fallow and unused.

We eventually found a new house and started another garden. In the first three months of the year 2000 we ripped up concrete, built soil on top of old asphalt and dug a bigger pond and wetland. We constructed a three-tier graywater treatment system, and set aside half the yard as a native and medicinal plant garden.

But while our backyard was taking shape, we were digging up strawberries and medicinal herbs from the evicted community gardens and put them in pots, because no new gardens had opened up since the real estate market got so tight in the mid nineties. Every lot that I had my eye on as a potential garden site got developed in that period. We focused on our native plant nursery and planted fruit trees in the curb strips of our neighborhood. Some survived. But it takes an

drawing by Lucha

apple tree ten years to bear good fruit, and only ten seconds to get knocked down with a bulldozer.

Gardens vs. Cops

It was spring, and guerrilla gardening was in the air. First, I got wind of the pitched battle for Jardín de la Esperanza, a 20-year-old garden in New York City's Lower East Side. In March, an email communique from activists in England reminded people to start seedlings to plant as part of Mayday Reclaim the Streets actions. Soon after, guerrilla gardeners called for people to bring "gardening tools, saplings, sprouted vegetables and all your friends" to Washington, D.C. during the protests against the IMF and World Bank. All these threads wound together in D.C. in the middle of April.

The day before the planned protest, fifty people walked away from a shouting match with police after federal marshals illegally raided the convergence center. While people planned lockdowns and confrontations with the power structure, we helped thirty neighborhood gardeners prepare beds and plant the spring crop in a community garden threatened by development.

My friend Aresh from New York City brought paper-mache dragonflies he'd made after the Esperanza garden was destroyed. He gave them to the kids to fly around the garden, scattering seeds of hope as they went.

A few days later, looking at pictures of Esperanza Garden in winter, hearing of its history and the struggle to save it, I understood the significance of those puppets. He flipped through pictures of people sitting around a fire among the dead plants and dormant trees, of the giant frog guarding the entrance to the garden with people locked inside to stop the bulldozers, of fifty fierce people locked down and lined up against the fence that cold spring morning. As he came to the last photographs, of the earth scraped bare, a fence painted with 'Esperanza garden once grew here,' he said "You could feel a huge rush of energy come surging out of the ground when they finally bulldozed the garden. All the years of work and play and laughter, all the care and children's voices, all the planning and struggle and people who were a part of the garden flew up into the sky and scattered, like seeds of hope. Some of those seeds got planted in D.C. last week. Maybe some took root in your life. The garden was destroyed, but the land remains."

Dumping Grounds Turned Green

I spent a year tracking down the stories that follow. In my apartment in Oakland, everlasting freeway noise in the background, I can see an old woman leaning out her window over fruit trees, cornstalks and chickens in her South Bronx garden. There's the Tacoma, Washington neighborhood where every patch of green is a garden and those gardens offer some sanctuary to those without homes. In Philly, three generations of women cultivate their plots under the railroad tracks in the long summer afternoons. Across the country, thousands of gardeners plant another season's crop on dumping grounds turned green.

With these stories, it becomes possible to peel back layers of concrete, of recent history, of economic boom and bust to imagine my neighborhood like that, a knot in a net drawing human people together and back to our roots. It's more than a mind trick: if we can see outside our time just long enough to know that another world is possible, then these stories become tools, guideposts, pieces of a puzzle.

This book is a resource guide for the gardeners I met and those like them. I've tried to compile some plans and practical ideas in the back, but there's no real basic gardening stuff here— how to plant, weed and harvest. The best way to learn to grow food is to buy some seeds, talk to the old lady with the big tomatoes in the garden on the corner and take her advice. What you can't learn from practice or from talking to people is available in the gardening section of your local library.

With these stories, it becomes possible to peel back layers of concrete, of recent history, of economic boom and bust to imagine my neighborhood like that, a knot in a net drawing human people together and back to our roots.

It is more difficult in this country and these times to find a patch of land to scatter seed on, and people to work it in the long term. In red-lined neighborhoods vacant lots are there for the taking, often full of toxic waste. In many areas, the younger generation lost traditions of cultivating the land. In some cities gentrification has turned land into a commodity far out of the reach of gardeners, where people have to work so much to pay rent that there's not time to produce food in a serious way. In others, car culture has so isolated people that they don't even know their neighbors.

But everyone's got to eat. And while gardens aren't a cure-all to the problems of economic racism and environmental injustice, unequal access to resources and an exploitative profit system, they can help us get by a little easier, give us space to breathe, to learn from the earth, and to begin to reweave relationships based on respect for the land and for the people around us.

Urban Gardens

mural at Thurgood Marshall High School, San Francisco, CA

Bronx, NY • Philadelphia, PA • Holyoke, MA • Tacoma, WA
Berkeley, CA • Havana, Cuba

This garden belongs to us, because we come and work here. The food that I give to these plants, the love, the time, the clothes I get dirty here every day—nobody will take away that.

—Melanie Rodriguez, Bronx gardener

These days, walking through a neighborhood I've never been in before, I keep my eyes open for a flash of green breaking the gray concrete scene: a peach tree hanging over a wall, rows of corn between two buildings, a patch of collard greens dug out of a lawn. I screech to a halt, get off my bike and peer through the chainlink fence, trying to see what's growing, to guess what continents their seeds came from and in what language a voice explained the process of sowing seed, bringing water and gathering the harvest.

Every city has these small patches of well-tended ground. They are the cultural and genetic seeds of the future cities we imagine: cities with gardens over parking lots, where people work together and eat well of what they've grown.

In conversations with gardeners across the country, I heard stories of taking control of abandoned lots in red-lined neighborhoods and turning them into living spaces that are places for people of different cultures and generations to gather. The gardens educate the youth, and in some places selling produce from urban gardens is giving them a viable alternative to the street economy. Urban gardens provide fresh produce that's much healthier than what the supermarkets sell, and takes very little cash investment to produce.

A Cape Verdean man in Roxbury, Massachusetts feeds all thirty of his grandchildren from the garden he grows on four vacant lots. His story is not so unusual. In Detroit, Michigan youth learn to farm with tractors on several-acre abandoned lots and sell the produce at Black Farmers' Markets. In Tucson, Arizona twelve Mexican women who live four miles from the nearest supermarket work together to grow produce out of their backyards. If we sift through these stories, and seek out this company in our own neighborhoods, we'll find more information on growing plants, saving seed, preserving food and sustaining soil than is contained in a whole library of gardening books.

Gardens Grow Healthy Communities

the Bronx United Gardeners

"We had to build these gardens. We needed and wanted these gardens. We grow healthy food in these gardens, but we do more than that. We don't just feed the children, we teach them love, respect, and non-violence," Cordelia Gilford, longtime South Bronx gardener explains.

Jim Austen concurs, "It's an escape for the kids from a lot of what they see around them, from a lot of what they experience." Most of the Bronx United Gardeners (BUG) seem to agree that one of the most important things that gardens do is provide a loving and respectful atmosphere for neighborhood children to learn and grow. "We know our children, and we know what they need. Giving them something special on their own block is the best thing we can do," says Tex Smith of 1306 Senior Citizen's garden. Many BUG gardeners have been active in starting garden programs through the science department at Middle School 158. "Its good for them to get out of their classroom and see and experience the world. Sitting in a desk while the sun is shining outside is boring. They learn more when they get to experience it for themselves, when they get to lead their own learning," one science teacher observes.

kids in a South Bronx Garden

place. Smith, 70, says "Older folks can relax and play cards, watch the younger kids and be part of the neighborhood. We also see how it makes our neighborhood safer, it makes it more beautiful, not such an eyesore. It also really brings people together. Doesn't matter race, age, anything."

And of course, there's the food. Sandra, a young mother feeds her one-year-old daughter food grown in the garden because "where else could I get such healthy tasty food for my baby? I can't go down to Manhattan, and even if I could, its expensive down there." By growing their own food, gardeners get healthy, often organic produce for the cost of their labor. "Vegetables I grow myself have always tasted better to me," says Ms. Mattie. "But I seem to remember when I was young that even food in the grocery store tasted better. Now its all just cardboard."

Not only do gardening programs teach kids skills and spark their interest, the gardens also show them a model of a different world.

"We are resources, I know who to speak to if your heat's been turned off. We share information and help each other get by."

"Its great for the kids in this neighborhood to see their neighbors really taking back control, and doing for themselves. The gardeners show kids around here that people can take power in to their own hands, and can create something special for the neighborhood," says Isabel Moore of Geneva McFadden garden. "Gardeners also frequently get very involved in issues affecting the neighborhood, like policing and tenants issues. It's good for kids to see active and courageous people in their midst, creating an alternative vision for the future. I think seeing gardens is empowering for kids growing up in such a harsh political climate that puts so little value on their well being."

Seniors are also enlivened by participating in the garden, and feel that it makes the neighborhood a better

Trees in the gardens clean the air, a much needed benefit in an area plagued by the highest pollution and asthma rates in the entire United States. According to Austen, "these gardens just improve the environment and make it more pleasant."

Gardens also provide spaces for local organizing around issues that affect the community. "We meet our neighbors here, and we talk about what goes on in the community," says Verna Judge. Gardens can be spaces for fundraisers, potlucks and meetings for a variety of neighborhood groups fighting to improve the area. "We are resources," explains Cordelia Gilford. "I know who to speak to if your heat's been turned off, where to go if you need help with this or that. We share information and help each other get by."

6

The Garden of Eatin'

cleo

I head south on my borrowed cruiser bike, past the urban renewal of downtown. Some blocks all the houses are boarded up or burnt out. Young people sitting on the stoops look me up and down for being on the wrong side of town. Many lots are vacant, and some of those have been planted with flowers and vegetables. At a corner store, I stop to look up Alta's number in the phone book. The young black Muslim woman behind the counter says, "Mrs. Felton? She lives down there on Taylor Street. Just ask around, you'll find her." I find my way to Taylor Street and ask a man standing on the corner where Mrs. Felton lives. "I been in jail three years and just got out this morning, but she used to live in that pink house right there," he says. Her daughter, Rosetta Little answers the door and invites me in. We spend four hours walking through the garden, talking about mustard greens and sweet corn, history, youth, decline and renewal in Philadelphia and across the country.

Alta Felton was born and raised in rural Virginia where she learned to garden from her mother and grandmother. She moved to Philadelphia in 1937, and has lived in the same house since the 1940s. Behind the row of houses, the Garden of Eatin' lies next to an elevated railroad line. A whole block of corn and fruit trees, collard greens, squashes and tomatoes grow in neat, square plots. A second, smaller garden down the block from Alta's house has been cultivated since 1938.

Alta Felton is 87. She stays healthy by eating collards, home-grown lima beans, sweet potatoes, corn, peppers, okra, tomatoes, peanuts, peaches and apples. She walks me through the half-block garden, leaning on a hoe she uses to cut weeds growing out of the path and between the white pickets of the fences around the plots.

At the south end of the garden I notice a legume I have never seen before growing in a neat plot of mustard greens and onions. "Lima beans," Alta explains. "An old man has grown them in this same spot for 35 years." On the edges of the garden paths, mustard greens, peas and peppers grow in stacks of tires as well as in beds. The ladies tell me that the tire stacks save space and help moderate day- and

At the north end of the garden women grow corn, beans, and sweet potatoes in a polyculture. Beans grow up the cornstalks, and the sweet potatoes spread to fill all the spaces between the corn rows. Among the intensively cultivated vegetable plots are plots overgrown with sweet potatoes. Alta harvests bags and bags of them from each small plot.

nighttime temperatures. They are also a good way to get rid of old tires in a neighborhood where garbage collection is not something one takes for granted.

All the gardeners are serious about producing lots of food. Rosetta Little says, "They all pay $10 a year for their plot, and leave with big bags full of food every time they come here." Alta grumbles that people in the neighborhood like to eat the food she and other gardeners give out, but that no one wants to put in the time and work necessary to grow food.

A Family Affair

The gardeners all live within a few blocks of the Garden of Eatin', and many of the plots belong to relatives. Rosetta has a plot, and her husband had one until his Alzheimer's got too bad. Alta's niece and granddaughter both have plots— her niece grows the best okra in the garden. Alta says that many of the people are good gardeners, but maintaining the paths and the common areas is left mostly to her.

At the north end of the garden women grow corn, beans, and sweet potatoes in a polyculture. Beans grow up the cornstalks, and the sweet potatoes spread to fill all the spaces between the corn rows. Among the inten-

Alta Felton (bottom) and her daughter Rosetta Little in the Garden of Eatin'

8

sively cultivated vegetable plots are plots overgrown with sweet potatoes. Alta harvests bags and bags of them from each small plot.

Alta was sick earlier in the year, so she hasn't been out in the garden as much this summer. She asked a man to water the garden down the block from her house (the one that's been there for 40 years) so it won't fall into disuse. I ask Rosetta about the changing dynamics of her neighborhood while she hoes her collard patch, which is very neat and free of weeds. She says kids come by with relatives, but as they get older they lose interest in the garden. She mentions a kid's gardening program starting up at a local senior center, and hopes that the young people who learn gardening from the seniors will become more engaged in the neighborhood gardens. But there is no youth gardening program at the Garden of Eatin'.

We walk by large piles of compost and wood chips donated by Philadelphia Green, a well-established community gardening association. Alta says that the City of Philadelphia also supports the garden. The land belongs to the city, but has been secure for years, because the City is glad to see South Philly's abundant vacant land used for gardens rather than drug deals and dumping.

"Everyone loves the fruit," Alta tells me, and it shows. Most plots have at least one fruit tree, some young and well-pruned, others twenty or thirty years old. Grapes grow over many of the fences.

One lady who Alta and her daughter both speak highly of planted a grape arbor, a peach tree and an old apple tree as well as berries and vegetables. She recently passed away, and they are turning her plot into a memorial garden.

I ask Alta and Rosetta why so many plots are abandoned. They say the folks who tend the Garden of Eatin' are of a much older generation. None are younger than 40, while most are in their 70s and 80s. As people die, their plots aren't taken over by the younger generation.

the Garden of Eatin'

Rosetta Little belongs the last generation to grow up in the rural South before World War II and the mechanization of agriculture displaced thousands of rural farmers. Alta and Rosetta were part of a wave of migration which brought agricultural knowledge to northern cities. There they carved out gardens to re-create the green spaces they grew up with.

But their city-born children lost the experience of growing food (even just a small garden) to wage jobs, sheer survival in a crumbling economy. This split occurs in many places. Youth don't take part because, as one gardener says, "We are part of a system which values glitter and money above living things." Many youth see little street value in their grandmothers' gardens. In South Philadelphia, and in many communities, there's the potential for traditional agricultural knowledge to be passed on while people of Rosetta's generation are still around. As I rode away from the Garden of Eatin', I saw the same young people sitting on the stoops, the vacant lots full of old tires and rubble, and I racked my brain to find the missing link. I had the feeling that if the youth stepped into the Garden of Eatin', it could be a part of empowering the community, creating opportunities for youth, and bringing the generations together.

Rosetta Little belongs the last generation to grow up in the rural South before World War II and the mechanization of agriculture displaced thousands of rural farmers. Alta and Rosetta were part of a wave of migration which brought agricultural knowledge to northern cities. There they carved out gardens to re-create the green spaces they grew up with.

The Street Value of Gardens

We stop to rest under a grape arbor in the center of the garden. In front of us is a large plot of freshly tilled ground that has stood vacant since its gardener passed away; the others plan to turn into an orchard.

Melanie's Garden

cleo

I spend six hours at Melanie's garden on Sherman and 163rd in the South Bronx one Thursday in September, working on banners for a Bronx United Gardeners rally. One banner shows a coqui (the frog that's the mascot of Puerto Rican boriqueño culture) sleeping in the shade of some palm trees. Later, I sit outside the garden gate with a neighbor watching the kids race their bikes up and down the sidewalks, the pretty high school girls walk up and down the street, while their *mamás* hang out the windows, leaning on Puerto Rican flags.

This neighbor tells me how he grew up around the corner and has moved from apartment to apartment over the years, but always on the same block. "Why move to some other block?" he says. "Here everyone knows each other. It's like a big family. If you go to some other neighborhood, you never know what will happen. If someone comes here from some other neighborhood and tries to fuck with me, all those people will come running down out of the buildings and beat the shit out of them."

Just then Melanie comes back with her grandson's stroller loaded down with Spanish food. We eat *arroz y frijoles y un carne muy rico* and we talked about her garden and her life growing up in Puerto Rico.

Melanie Rodriguez

Two years ago, here, to this garden came a girl who used to live next to me. And asked for two dollars. And I give it to her but before I gave it to her, maybe out of curiosity for me, I asked her, "What do you need the two dollars for?" She says "I'm going to tell you the truth. I can't lie." She says, "I'm a prostitute. I use these two dollars to go downtown to my job." I got so upset. I said, "Are you happy with this life?" She said, "I am not happy, even though I'm making all kind of money, because I'm on drugs." And I say, "Young girl like you, pretty girl like you, you're going to turn all these opportunities down and do the worst thing—prostitution." She didn't say a word, she said 'Thank you Melanie for the two dollars,' and she left.

A year later she came back here. I saw this nurse. She hugged me, kissed me. "Do you remember me?," she said. I said no, because so many people come. She said, "Do you remember the girl you lent the two dollars?" and I say yes. She said, "You know what? From the day you said drugs and prostitution was not the best world, that they destroy life," and I say, "Oh yes I do, now I remember what I told you." "Well I tell you what," she said, "I quit that job, quit that kind of work, graduated from nursing school, and now I'm a registered nurse." She came with the white shoes and the uniform. And that day I told her, "You made me the happy day in my life. I never expected that a person I talked to could begin to change that same day, and I'm glad and I'm proud of you and I hope that you can remember me and turn that around again."

I told her life is short, and if I did it, you could too, because I'm coming from a poor family. Not poor like I'm asking for a piece of bread on the streets, but poor because I never have $10 in my hand. That's what I call poor. In Puerto Rico I lived in a beautiful house with a good family, a lot of food, and a lot of land—68 acres. My father was a farmer. Very good too. He worked like a horse, from 6 o'clock in the morning to 6 o'clock in the afternoon, to give us education, to give us everything. And it was a very different life. That was life. This is not life. This is suffering suffering suffering from the minute you get up to the time you go to bed, because you don't know what's going to happen.

In Puerto Rico, we went here, there, everybody was nice, no fresh people, no stealing. All of them went to college, except my brother. But he was a very good musician. My family were musicians—all of them. My sister sings. My father made guitars. They raised us all together in a big big huge house, with a balcony, on a hill—beautiful hill. We had cows, pineapples, tomatoes, eggplants, peas, *plátanos*, a lot of bananas—green, yellow—too much! He used to sell a lot of *yautia*—it's like potatoes, you have to take it from the ground. *Yautia* is delicious—the white one especially. I used to sell them by the sack—three dollars for a sack, or for two or three bunches of bananas.

drawing by Rubisel

This was my first garden here in New York. I always dreamed to have a garden here. I felt empty. I wasn't accustomed to living in an apartment. I don't care how much furniture you have. I always told my husband I wanted to have land in Puerto Rico, *land* in Puerto Rico, and have some rivers, trees, horses, everything. Until I got this place. This was my chance to develop what I wanted.

When I got this my mother was about to pass away. I told her, "I'm going to have a nice garden." Neither my father nor my mother could see it, because they passed long before.

Do other people from the neighborhood help you?

They donate things—this table, paints. In the beginning I let people come and garden. And they would just take my tomatoes. But they are members, yes, they give me support, and if anything happened to me, they would carry it on.

The kids! Sometimes I have to close the door. I teach them to plant. *(She motions to a boy and a fruit tree)* I taught that boy to plant that, and it's his tree. These children love me like a grandmother. They all call me that, *abuelita.*

When I go back to Puerto Rico I'm going to bring back a small green banana plant. I saw one in a garden on 3rd Avenue. This lady there brought pieces of the root of the banana plant from Puerto Rico. Last week I passed by there and I said "Lady, lady, this is a banana plant, no?" And she said, "Yes, banana and plantain." I said "What? Sell me one." She said $35. I didn't come back because I wanted to have a couple pieces, not just one, and if I'm going to have three, you know $75, I better just go to Puerto Rico and bring one back. It won't cost me nothing.

That peaches tree— *oooh!* A lot of peaches. I let the neighbors come but they grab everything. You don't have to give, they take. I have apples, peaches, prunes. Green Guerrilla gave me all kinds of trees. I was crazy to get that willow tree.

What would happen if you planted trees on the street?

Everyone knows the big tree growing next to the sidewalk is my tree. That's a $300 tree, because you need a license to plant a tree. You can't just open the street like that. You need a license to plant a tree. They know

My uncle came to the US, and then he went back to Puerto Rico and told my mother there were more opportunities to work and go to school here. I was studying to become a nurse. In 1948 I moved here, and it was not the same as today. In those days you could sleep on the streets and nobody would touch you. I came and I married here, and I went to school, because I had no english, and if you don't have english here you have nothing.

Since my childhood my mother gave me the opportunity to have my piece of land in the back of the house. She said, "This is for you." She used to have pigs and chickens. I started planting, and my mother found out I had a good sense with plants. I remember I saw my mother digging in the dirt, fertilizing—I learned all these things from my mother.

In all those years, from when you came from Puerto Rico to when you started this garden, did you garden in other places?

that I'll fight with them if they touch my tree. I fight with the city all the time and they respect me, because I get mad.

That's what we do in Oakland, we tear up the pavement to plant apples, plums and redwoods.

You did? No, we have to call the parks department, and the Parks Department had a commission from the city. To make the hole is a big job, and bulldozer has to come to bring out the dirt and open the cement.

The three guys who helped me put this tree down, two are dead already and one is about to die. They got sick with *la SIDA*—- HIV. They took drugs. I tried to help them as much as I could but when they are deep in drugs there's nothing you can do. I tried to help them to change. You can't change people.

My neighborhood is deep in drugs. Everywhere you put your eyes somebody is doing something. I have more than 25 kids here. I feel sorry. Because I never smoked. If you show me a marijuana cigarette I probably say yes, ok, but I don't know what is drugs really. I don't have that experience. If the garden helps me save five of these kids' lives from drugs I will be happy.

I'm not going to lay down on the street with nothing, no, I'm going to lay down in front of this garden. And if you remove me I will come back again and lay down. Or I'll kill one of them, I don't care.

Tell me about when they tried to bulldoze this garden.

Oh yes, I lost 15 pounds. After 17 years they told me they were going to take away my garden, they were going to bulldoze my garden. For a parking lot! I went there, and I was on television, and we had a rally too. I kept repeating "Over my dead body." First you have to go through my body, because I'm going to lay down. You can kill me. That's what I said. Everyone was laughing and screaming.

I'm not going to lay down on the street with nothing, no, I'm going to lay down in front of this garden. And if you remove me I will come back again and lay down. Or I'll kill one of them, I don't care.

So how did this garden finally get saved? Did you have to lie down in front of the bulldozer?

What happened is that Mr. Calderon and Mr. Coppa from the Trust for Public Lands visited me. They saw the problems we have with the kids and the street. They saw how the kids loved it here. And they found out that I spent 17 years, and $45,000 making it.

So they bought it. But now the question is, at the last meeting I went to, they said that in two years they're going to let this garden be our garden, with the purpose of community service. They said in another six or seven months they're going to give us a copy of the deed to this garden. The garden no longer belongs to the city. It belongs to the community. As long as I live, as long as my children live, the city can't have this garden.

So now you're fighting for all the other gardens in the Bronx?

I feel sorry for the other people whose gardens are in danger, because you work for seven or ten years just to have [the city] destroy your property. To me this garden is mine. It's a part of my life. I come here sometimes seven o' clock in the summer, and then at seven or eight o' clock I go home, take a shower and go to sleep.

After all that work here, after all that money here, you don't have nothing. That's why I started losing weight, the moment I heard. My friend told me, "Your garden is endangered." I said, "What!?!" She said, "Your garden's going to be in an auction." I started losing weight that minute. My garden, my children, my work, my time, for what? For a parking lot, for people to come here, to sell drugs.

Ana down the street has a beautiful garden. Small—but very well organized. My garden and her garden are saved. The rest? Hmmph!

Between you and me, this garden belongs to us, because we come and work here. The food that I give to these plants, the love, the time, the clothes I get dirty here every day; time, earth, work, material. Nobody will take away that.

What advice would you give to gardeners in other cities whose gardens are threatened?

My first advice is to keep it nice. If you keep it nice, and you really involve the community and the children, I don't see how they can take it away from you. When I told everyone around here what was going on, they came and they said No. No no no.

(Melanie walks over to the banner drying in the small patch of sun that filters between the tall buildings.)

So what we're going to do here, tomorrow, we gotta write something here. What are we going to write?

What you said before. ¿Como se llama este animal?

Coqui.

Let the coqui rest in peace, no? But that sounds like he died.

You don't need to say "Rest in peace." We could say "Let the coqui sleep long." *Hasta el coqui duerme tranquilo en el jardín, no removarlos!*

the People's Garden

an interview with Terry Compost

cleo

In 1969, the University of California at Berkeley tore down a square block of a neighborhood. The Victorian houses held activists, students and working people. The University had used eminent domain to buy the houses, because it claimed it would build a dorm on the land. But many guessed that the real intention was to disrupt the radical culture that continued in the tradition of the Free Speech Movement. Thousands answered the call for action and created People's Park on what used to be their neighborhood.

The University responded by calling in the National Guard who eventually succeeded in erecting a fence around the newly claimed free space. A few years later the people tore the fence down, and it has stayed down ever since. These days, the park is a haven for youth, people passing through town and those without homes. Food Not Bombs and the Hari Krishnas serve free vegetarian meals daily, the free box redistributes clothes. For now the University says they're interested in keeping the park as open space, though in the past they have tried to turn it into everything from volleyball courts to parking to student housing. Legally, there is nothing to prevent them from doing this. But, as Terry Compost , who has coordinated the garden for the last eight years says, "The park rises to its full glory when it's being attacked. Whenever the University threatens the park, people come out of the woodwork to defend it."

At the east end of People's Park is a grove of redwoods and other native plants. In the center is a wide, often muddy lawn facing a stage where Food Not Bombs serves every day at 2:30 pm. Behind the stage are the dozen raised beds and small orchard of plum, apple, fig, pear and lemon trees that make up the People's Park community garden. There is a children's plot with radishes, lettuce and tomatoes, a perennial herb garden, beds with vegetables growing in them and beds full of flowers. "Betsy, a street lady who died, planted roses here that are still blooming. There are spirits in this soil. There are ghosts deep in this land."

The gardeners range from local apartment-dwellers who are "hip to the People's Park myth," to homeless people who eat the vegetables they grow. "There have been so many people over the years who have done something

in the garden. It's this bizarre group project that stretches back into history," says Terry Compost.

While only a half-dozen people have plots in the garden, many more eat the fruit off the trees as they pass through. This fruit has served as handy ammunition during confrontations with the cops over the years. The garden also hosts activities such as classes on the medicinal uses of weeds, plant identification with middle school kids and repainting the murals on different walls. While these events attract the student and middle-class population of Berkeley, the garden and park are used mostly by the homeless, by street kids, and by the youth on the basketball courts.

"There's a lot of support out there among the wingnuts," Terry says. In spite, or more likely because of this constant presence of park-users, vandalism is not a problem in the unfenced garden. In fact, Terry says, the greatest damage occurs when the groundspeople weed-wack. There's no waiting list for a garden plot if you don't mind the chaos that comes from gardening in a very public place.

The gardeners at People's Park grow less food than other gardeners I visited. It seems that the garden's social element, educational programs and its function

"Betsy, a street lady who died, planted roses here that are still blooming. There are spirits in this soil. There are ghosts deep in this land."

as a refuge for the homeless have eclipsed serious food production here. Terry Compost agrees that the garden could use more people. But the garden is intimately connected to the history of the Park. "It's a big story, which has involved a lot of people and social movements over the years," Terry says. "It's the only turf left around here that pretends to be common land."

Guadalupe Gardens

an interview with Carrie Little

This neighborhood has always been a hub area for taking care of people on the streets. There's a soup kitchen right behind us, and there's the largest food bank in the county right behind it, and down below us is Nativity House which is a day center for homeless people. There's this migratory pattern that happens, and with that comes a lot of drug dealing and there's a lot of empty lots. That bothered us, because shit was going on in those places. So one by one we started taking them over.

La Grande Garden

It's just where a one-acre garden needs to be. It's in the middle of a Vietnamese neighborhood, and there are a lot of Hispanics, a lot of Russians, and everyone hangs on their fences and watches and says, "Wow. What are you doing?" Having that urban connection is so rich

Two Vietnamese guys with a lawnmowing business dump grass clippings. I've invited them to come in and garden, and they haven't done it, but what they love to do is come in and harvest my weeds: chickweed, smartweed, and another weed that looks very similar to something they grow. I put pumpkins on the end of these beds and they came cascading this way—because of the compost they just went nuts. We had 75 to 80 pound pumpkins.

Kevin Putney Memorial Garden

This is the first garden we took over. We named it after Kevin Putney, who lived on this site out of his car. He cleared an area next to his vehicle and laid out an inviting living room scene complete with chairs, tables and a couch. He called it the 'colored peoples' park.' I asked him once if a white sassy gal like myself would be welcome into his "park." He gave me one of his famous grins and asked me if I were a color. "Sure I am—a little pink, red, dirt brown," I responded and he said, "Well come in then, this is for 'colored' people only!"

Initially the people who owned the lot said, "Oh, no, you can't come and garden here," and we said, "But you have a disaster going on here, and there's drug activity, and people are dumping." They were really reluctant to allow us to do it, but when we cleaned it up they said, "Oh, well that's nice."

And then they sold it out from under us— we had no idea they were going to do it. It happened a year ago today. So we no longer garden this site. A corporate entity bought this piece and the piece next door and they sold it to a developer who plans on building 300 condos. We had no warning.

Gene's Garden

Gene's garden, next to the Guadalupe House, has been cultivated the longest. It used to be tended by people who lived on the streets. A guy named Gene used to live in the center of this garden, and lived out of his tent and had a campfire and just really welcomed people to join in. I didn't get the honor of meeting him—he died before I got here—but you can really sense him in the special magic here.

The Corner Park

In 1995 a man died of a drug overdose in this area. We had been gardening primarily the part of the neighborhood around the Guadalupe house, and said, "Wait a minute, that can't be happening in our neighborhood," and we started shifting things over here. We talked to the guy who owned the land, and he said we could take it over, so we got the park site and the lot next door and got a big grant to really turn it into more of a farm to support the CSA.

You couldn't even see—it was solid blackberry and brush, and we macheted through here and realized there were all these cherry trees. When all the debris was hauled out, we discovered that the place where the man had died was really very beautiful. Our neighbor could finally see the side of his house, and said, "Gee, I'd better paint it."

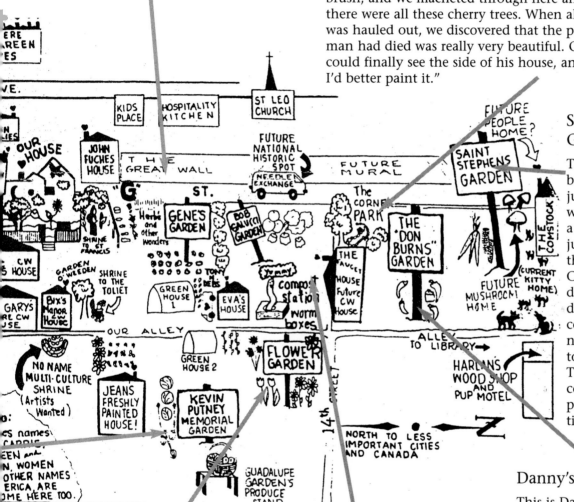

St. Stephen's Garden

This was a really beautiful garden that just got mortally wounded. There was a building there that just got burned to the ground. St. Leo's Church let the fire department burn it down so it would cost them nothing, never mind all the toxic waste involved. Their solution was to cover the garden in plastic, and the plastic caught on fire.

Danny's Garden

This is Danny's Garden. Danny is one of our happy stories, because he literally lived in the woodpile for 3 years. He didn't talk to anybody, until finally I came around and said, "Hey, want to garden?" The garden is his baby. He just expanded this year, so this is new territory for him. Those purple Brussels sprouts are beautiful.

Flower Garden

I had all the sites tested for lead. There were lead levels in all of them, but nothing really dangerous. But the site where the flower garden is had really high levels of lead, and had horsetails all over it. I didn't bother with doing cover crops or removing the soil, because it's just flowers.

Galuchi garden

There's growing space up above, and a compost site below. The neighborhood likes to bring their brush and leaves, so we chip it all up and crank out compost like it's going out of style. In the spring we bring in a lot of compost, and in the fall we take everything out of the gardens and plant a cover crop. A cover crop's a wonderful thing.

Dragonfly's Garden

an interview with Kathi Kinney, Earth Mother

The 59th Street Garden is a well-known spot in North Oakland. It's a rare green oasis, an unfenced community garden full of fruit trees, towering Jerusalem Artichokes, Hops vines and a sweet-scented wild section planted with dozens of medicinal herbs. I'd been there often, during the day to escape the throb of the city and by night to sit on the worm-bin benches under the oak tree and listen to the crickets play their lonesome songs. Then I met Kathi Kinney and the gardeners she works with, and over the course of several hot Tuesday mornings, she passed on her story.

Kathi Kinney

I've been in gardens all my life. I'm 53, and when I was six I knew that I was gonna play in the dirt, climb trees and plant flowers and herbs, because it made me feel good. I grew up with people who cared about money and material things, and they weren't very healthy. But when I'd bring a plant around they would transform, for a minute, until they realized "I can't sell this to buy no Cadillac."

My grandma liked a lot of plants, but most of the rest of them were materialistic, you know, "thing hungry." And most of them have died off from cancer, from being greedy, from their diet, and from the way they held on to stuff. They would always laugh at me, and I'm here healthy, so go figure that.

Echinacea in Kathi Kinney's backyard garden in Richmond, CA

When my mother died, I got a call from a surgeon who cut on a lot of my other aunts who all died of cancer. And he said, "Well you know Kathleen, you need to set up an appointment with me." And I said, "You know what Dr. So-and-so, I ain't got nothing on my body that you want." And that was it.

I had a grandmother who was really into herbs and stuff, and I have a lot of recipes, but other than that it just went from spirit within me, which is intuition, which guides me still.

How did you get involved with the garden here?

I've been here since last August, about a year now. I had a meeting with Daniel Green. He had heard about me because I was the lead educator at SLUG, and he was saying, "Why don't you come work for us. It's 80% gardening and 20% office." And I said, no, because that would be 80% office and 20% outside, and I just couldn't do that. So then six months later he came an said, "Okay, we have somebody who will do the office stuff." So I'm outside all the time. I can't deal with being indoors. I can't do the politics, I can't do the pettiness, I just can't do it. It's not normal. We're not supposed to be in an office like that eight to ten hours a day.

So I'm out here, and I teach out here. We have eight interns who are in transition, trying to deal in this society that's just crazy. Frankly I don't know why they want too come back here, to society (*laughs*). I'm teaching them about growing their own food, growing their own medicine. I do plant ID with them. We interact with the community. People come; on Tuesdays and Thursday mornings we have a group of autistic young people who come. They just planted some cucumbers, swiss chard and bok choi and they loved it! I'm out here cultivating people as well as plants, you know? And it's wonderful.

One of the interns wasn't feeling too well this morning, and she just went on about her situation, and I said, "No, just think joy. Just be out here, and whatever

16

you're going through, just think joy, and it'll be okay." Look at where you are. Look at this— you see the dragonflies, they're all over the place, so we must be doing something right.

The Garden

I don't want it to be all this order. I just like the way it is. I know I need to take the grass out of the beds, but it's a lot of work. People come to help, and I don't just want to put them on weeds. I want to teach them how to identify the plants so they know why we're talking about this one, and leaving in that one. That's important.

Who eats this food?

The participants and interns take it, and we give it to the community. We have a good following now. At first a lot of people thought is was a private garden. I don't think it was really inviting to them. Now they see me, I'm on the street and say, "Come on in." So now people are starting to trickle in. This isn't privately owned. Nothing should be privately owned, really. It's for everybody.

I tell them what we're growing. You know, "African-Americans really like collards," so we got collards, as well as swiss chard, mustard greens, corn, kale, butter lettuce, potatoes and yakon, which is a tuber, you eat the root. We grow peppers, tomatoes and zuchini of course. We have lemon, apple and fig trees, and grapes, strawberries, blackberries, raspberries. And butterflies. Look at that swallowtail. Pretty, huh? So we're doing something good.

Have you had problems with people coming in and harvesting the wrong stuff?

Well sometimes, like with this clary sage, someone came and dug up the whole plant and left the hole. I had to do a little workshop on how to harvest greens because people would take the whole plant instead of just the leaf. But other than that, this food's here to be eaten.

Before I started working here, neighborhood people didn't know there were classes being given, because I didn't know there were classes being given, because I don't think [the people who used to run the garden] did outreach into the community. I go to the churches, the laundromat, the stores. I see people on the street and I'm like, "Hey, come on in." I go to the check cashing place, restaurants, all those places around here. I just stick my head in and say, "You know, we have a garden. Come help!"

A lot of people have this idea that if you have a community garden, you have to have a fence around it.

I know. I don't want to have a fence here. We were having some problems with the local drug dealer. I do what I have to, periodically, to keep him away. But it's worth it, because I don't want a fence, because I'd have to come here, unlock it, then come back and lock it up again. What kind of a thing is that? I don't like the gate idea. That's part of ownership, the American way or whatever. I don't think it's necessary.

Growing Medicinal Herbs

What's missing from a lot of gardens now are herbs. There are more than 100 plants that can save your life!

Kathi Kinney

Instead of monopolizing on this fact and selling to people, why not teach communities how to grow their own? You can grow some of the most powerful medicines known to humankind. I call these plant "super-medicines". Why spend lots of money on prescription drugs, which are mostly souped-up versions of what you can get from the earth...

Herbs can be included in your diet— not just to season foods, but to maintain and restore great health. This goes for long-term debilitating diseases also. It's easy to grow your own "pharmacy". Most herbs need lots of sun but a few (borage, yerba buena, sweet woodruff, japanese parsley, mint, lemon balm, garlic chives, ginger, english chamomile, chervil) can tolerate shade when the Sun is at its hottest. People coming to assist in the garden are often surprised that herbs can be trees, shrubs, flowers, vines, and ferns. I also let people know that an herb is any plant that seasons food or has a medicinal use. The following herbs should be in everyone's garden. Or, if not in the garden, in the kitchen: **garlic** (a whole-body tonic, boosting the immune system— a powerful natural antibiotic); **ginger** (used for dizziness, motion sickness, nausea, arthritis, and as a heart and blood tonic). Together with garlic, ginger is one of the best all-around herbs! **Horseradish** (taken with food, aids digestion. Used as a nasal decongestant and to relieve rheumatic distress; a natural antibiotic); **Cayenne pepper** (good for everything from high blood pressure/heart disease to stomach upset and ulcers), a great tonic; **Chives** (lower blood pressure); **Dill** (increases milk production for nursing mothers. Good for gas, colic, and stomach disorders); **Anise** (similar to dill, increases milk production for nursing mothers, treats gastric problems); **Bay Leaf** (relieves indigestion); **Onion** (as a regular part of your diet, helps control blood pressure—both high and low— as well as heart ailments); **Parsley** (a diuretic to use while dieting to lose weight, considered one of the finest herbs for treating kidney complaints). I let people know that they have to take responsibility for their own health, especially with the costs of drugs these days. I could go on and on about the wonderful qualities of herbs, but, I think everyone gets the picture! It's time to take back our lives!

– Kathi Kinney

We all have locks at home, although I took all the doors down in my house. I want it open. I don't want locks and doors and restrictions.

Growing Good Medicine

My grandmother had a recipe where she chops up comfrey and she puts it in a dark bottle. She leaves it in there for two years, and she gets this wonderful amber oil from it.

I go to the churches, the laundromat, the stores, the check cashing place, restaurants. I just stick my head in and say, "You know, we have a garden. Come help!"

The water goes down into that marshy here area and elcampane, valerian, milkweed, St. John's wort, and evening primrose are growing there.

This is a bishop flower. The nomads in Africa use it like we use sunscreen. They eat the root and it protects their skin from the sun. You never hear about skin cancer in Africa. I need to cut back this horehound, but I don't want to do it until I'm ready to use it.

What part of it do you use?

You can use it all, the leaves and the seeds. You can make a good cough syrup with honey and garlic.

Dragonflies

Steve, an intern at the garden, joins the conversation:

I enjoy the garden, it's outside, you get to deal with nature, so it's cool. Each person has one or two beds, and you just clear it out, decide what to plant.

Come here, dragonfly. He's gonna land on my finger, watch.

Kathi begins again:

They come because of the garden, because of the water and because of the aphids. They eat those things. We're not doing any spraying. This is the way it's supposed to be. We're supposed to have all kind of critters. They're really pretty, they'll come kind of close to you too. Some of the kids don't know what dragonflies are, before they come here.

My grandmother used to tell me if I wasn't good, they'd sew my ears up. So I learned to respect them. She would say, "You're having bad thoughts. The dragonflies are out there," and I cleared them thoughts up.

Teaching

I'm gonna be giving a series of classes like plant ID, herbs you can use, and I'm gonna do a special class on

alternatives to lawns, because I think we should not be dealing with lawns. The maintenance! One of my jobs was I was a gardener at San Francisco State, and they put me on the football field. I said, "This is not gonna work!" 'Cause I'll mess it up. I said, "I'll have zuchinis and cornfields. I'm not gonna take care of any lawn." You know, this garden was a house at one point. Isn't this better than putting another house here?

What's your larger vision, beyond this garden?

I know this has been said so much, but I would like to get some of the vacant lots and make them into gardens, even if it's just for a little while. People always trippin' on the value of property. It will up their value. We can work with private people who own lots and say, "We're gonna beautify your property, and you can get

Kathi (right) and an intern at the 59th Street Garden

food." You'd be surprised how many people will go for that, because you create a sanctuary. People think of Oakland and Berkeley and Richmond as so awful. I don't think of it that way. I go from a point of the glass being half full, instead of half empty. Because if the place is so bad, start from yourself, and get yourself together and go out and spread that. Don't talk about the other person. You do something. So this would help.

I'd like to eventually start a place of healing in all cities and all countries. You could train people, and have this place where people could come, and commune with plants, commune with nature, learn about medicine plants. It's so simple. And we're so busy.

I'd like to have a program with kids out here, an intergenerational program with kids, their parents and their grandparents, because we think we're so different, and we're not, we want the same things. And when you bring people together you can see that— that we're all one. We really are all one.

Food Not Lawns

a grassroots education project

text and photos by Heather Humus

The American lawn could feed the world if people were willing to turn it over for fruit and nut trees, vegetables and herbs. A lawn of 1000 to 1500 square feet could be planted with 100-200 edible and beneficial plant species within six months, and become a lush perennial "food forest" within three years. Yet in every city, town and industrial park in the country, fertile soil suffocates under thousands of acres of rolling lawn.

If we are to achieve community autonomy from the corporate regime— if we are to bring down the machines of destruction— we must establish fully sustainable, ecologically sound food and education networks at home. Who controls our food controls our bodies. Who controls our education controls our minds.

Food Not Lawns started in early 1999 in a 6000-square-foot city lot. A few gardener-activists were inspired to grow some food for Food Not Bombs. We'd cooked at our house every Sunday for years and wanted to "close the loop" by growing good organic food to cook and serve. Five people cleared out all the old trash and blackberry brambles, built some compost piles, and started what became the Food Not Lawns permaculture education garden. This garden, home to more than 350 species of edible, rare and native plants is a successful demonstration of an organic, low-maintenance, food-producing perennial garden. From here we distribute seeds and plants throughout the bioregion. We also host regular classes and projects in the garden.

We were lucky to find this land to garden on. We squatted it for a year before the city caught on, and by the time they wanted to scrutinize us, we were able to give them a tour. The plants spoke for themselves and the garden remains. Many gardeners in similar situations have been bulldozed, arrested or both. I do not know how to overcome the increasing industrial demand for land, only that I must continue to fight it.

We were also willing to garden in 75% shade; the garden is surrounded on all sides by fruit trees. It is extremely useful to know about food plants that are shade tolerant, drought tolerant and cold hardy.

Food Not Lawns is currently establishing a non-profit, with the intention of setting up a low-cost, rural-urban permaculture exchange school that is a working example of sustainability.

Education

We sponsor a permaculture design course for low-income neighbors— the first of its kind in the US. We are implementing class design projects all over the neighborhood. We also host weekly hands-on workshops on seed saving, biodynamics, kids' gardening, community organizing, composting, guerrilla gardening, sustainable horticulture, water conservation, appropriate technology, and other topics. Hosting workshops is simple: get some books and supplies together and start building this stuff at your house;

photo by Greg Jalbert

The average American can identify 300 corporate logos but only about 17 plants. This is pathetic. There are 30,000 edible plant species known to humans. How many are in your diet?

post some flyers around town announcing when and where you'll be working and people will come to help you. Some of them will know less than you do about whatever the topic is, and some people will inevitably show up who know more. In this way, we have a skills-intensive, result-producing activity that also expands the community. The Dirt Church Distribution is another one of our educational activities. We edit the Weed Lover, a sustainable horticulture reader and distribute how-to manuals & resource lists.

Local food: Hooking it up

In addition to ongoing maintenance and improvement of the Food Not Lawns educational garden, we coordinate volunteer work parties at local organic farms. We have three greenhouses where we propagate native and unusual edibles for distribution to the community. (Two of these have bamboo and duct-tape frames- simple and cheap to make!) We also facilitate a monthly Gardeners' Market, to encourage networking between local growers, activists and other community members.

The emphasis, of course, is on the plants themselves: propagating them and getting them into the ground wherever possible. They will outlive us, most of them, and we owe it to them to give them the chance to.

Some of the results of this work are bioregional beautification, increased biodiversity, increased sustainability, stronger community, more and better quality food and health, independence, autonomy and any hope in hell of survival.

Access

In many cities there are now community gardens and food co-ops, as people realize the need to re-establish a connection to their food sources. Ideas about permaculture, deep ecology and biodiversity are finally beginning to take hold, and many education centers have been established. But the average working person today is either too poor, too busy or both to take advantage of permaculture courses, which usually cost from $700-$1200 for a 2-week course. Organic food, heirloom seed and alternative education

top: Fruit trees and compost for the front yard orchard

middle: Turning lawns into food with Food Not Lawns

bottom: Mini orchard boy love

are equally inaccessible for most families. As a result, exposure to ecologically sound alternatives is often limited to activists, students and well-to-do people. Many mainstream, working-class families are never even aware that there are simple, affordable ways to live an ecologically sound life.

To counter this trend, all Food Not Lawns activities are conducted on an equal-opportunity basis, with people of all race, class, age and ability encouraged to attend. No one is ever turned away for a lack of funds, and childcare or kid classes are offered whenever possible.

Dietary Diversity

The average American can identify 300 corporate logos but only about 17 plants. This is pathetic. There are 30,000 edible plant species known to humans. How many are in your diet?

There are thousands of low-maintenance, high-yield plants that will grow with little input and produce lots of food for the community. As activists, we cannot afford to spend all of our time cultivating our own food supply. We must be able to grow large amounts of highly nutritious food, sustainably, and then move on to the issues at hand.

Is it a greater service to society (and to the Earth) to set up a self-sufficient lifestyle model to work from, or to participate in a movement against the hand that feeds us? We must disengage from corporate control; we can voluntarily withdraw from the consumer society, and use the waste to recreate Paradise.

In order to achieve this goal, we must be willing to diversify our diets to include the plants which will thrive in a permaculture environment (no such thing as a noxious weed!). Jerusalem artichoke, daylily, kudzu, akebia, black walnut, plum, filbert, kale, burdock, chickory, mustard, rhubarb, hops, raspberries, blueberries, blackberries, horseradish, garlic, chard, leeks and nettles are just a few. These plants are easy to grow, easy to propagate, and highly nutritious. There are literally tens of thousands more waiting to be discovered by you. What better way to topple the ivory towers than with a wild food invasion?

About now you're probably saying, "I don't wanna eat Jerusalem artichokes, aren't they invasive?" Well, I believe it's truly indicative of our sadly brainwashed selves that we fear diversity so much that we'll forsake the very survival of our species to avoid it. Our fore-mothers definitely ate the native sunchokes. Lots of them. They probably ate several other sunflower tubers as well. In fact, in the Helianthus genus there are at least 40 species of plants with edible buds, seeds and tubers. You could start with ten of these, planting them on street corners across the city...

Jerusalem Artichoke (⅓ natural size).

Closing the Loop

Remember, it is essential to maintain the soil fertility. For every calorie we take out as fruit or vegetable, we need to return one to the soil. To help with this, we cruise the back doors of the stores and cafes in town and pick up their vegetable waste for compost piles and sheet mulching. We also use urine and lots of compost teas.

Every city is overflowing with waste materials than can become fertility and eventually food supply. It is important to salvage these materials, keeping them out of the landfill and in use. This type of activity also inadvertently educates the people who see you doing it!

We also scatter clover and vetch seed (both excellent green manures) often and generously. These are nitrogen fixers, and you can harvest the seed yourself or order it in bulk for cheap.

Evening Primrose (⅓ natural size).

Chicory, or Succory (blanched). (⅓ natural size).

Plants

All life on earth, and especially human life, is dependent on plants. Plants make all of the oxygen we use to breathe. Plants provide food, fuel, fiber, medicine, shelter, etc. If one is to re-connect with nature, the fastest route is via the plants.

Anyone can grow plants, anywhere. There are plants that like shade, sun, hot, cold, dry, wet, loud and quiet places. Read books. Ask your neighbors. Read seed packs and the little tags in the pots at the nursery. Go to a botanical garden. Grow a botanical garden. Grow a kinship garden, in pots in the bathroom window. Start now, you can read the rest of this later! Pick a genus and start collecting every species in that genus. I like edible ones like Helianthus, Prunus, Allium, Rubus...

Eat what you grow and grow what you eat. Distribute the surplus. Build rocket stoves & hayboxes. Build rain catchment. Build ponds and swales everywhere. Recycle all water always. Compost your trash. Don't expect others to be responsible for your food and waste. She who eats well, lives well.

Learn how to do more stuff and teach your neighbors. Host a study group. Grow seeds. The plants are evolving constantly, adapting to conditions and to their own metamorphoses. There is infinite wisdom in their teachings, but we must be willing to listen. The gardens can sustain us all. There are millions of seeds blowing in the wind wanting to grow.

One plan for a forest garden in the Northwest

drawing by Greg Jalbert

Nuestras Raices

Walking towards the Centro Agricola run by Nuestras Raices, down blocks and blocks of old brick buildings, I pass markets selling sweet-sour tamarind candy and plantain chips. I cross two wide canals, left over from the days when Holyoke was a mill town. Just past the second canal I see a small patch of vegetables growing in front of the YMCA, one of many gardens started by Nuestras Raices. I recognize the Centro by the huge greenhouse filled with banana and other tropical plants facing a small plaza. The office itself is full of focused energy. Kids do their homework and stamp envelopes while a young woman and her daughter bring me down to one of the gardens.

The garden takes up most of one block, and is bordered by four-story brick apartment buildings. It is late summer, and all of the plots are bursting with beans, tomatoes, chiles and some plants I don't recognize. In fast Puerto Rican Spanish, the gardeners introduce me to traditional Puerto Rican crops. They offer me different chiles to taste, and laugh when the sweet flavor of the *aji dulce* lulls me into taking a big bite of a hot yellow pepper. In a mix of Spanish and English, they tell me the story of Nuestras Raices.

Margarita, Nuestras Raices member

"Most of our population are Puerto Rican. Every time we make a big party we roast a pig— that's

how we use this garden here.

This first garden that I'm going to show you is the largest of our gardens. It was the first garden we made. It was started three years ago, and it's called La Finquita ("the farm"). Eight years ago there was a building here that was burned. The local residents got together and asked the city for the lot so they could do something like this.

A lot of the people in Nuestra Raices are rural gardeners from Puerto Rico, so they got together, and this is what they have accomplished. So far we have five gardens. There's 32 families in these gardens and they just grow their stuff. They make what we call *sofrito* which is a condiment that we put on beans and rice. If we're gonna make a stew, we put *sofrito*. It's easier for them

because it's really expensive to buy, plus it has preservatives when you buy it in the store so the food doesn't taste the same.

They also have tomatoes, peppers, eggplants, sweet peppers, cabbage, zucchini, lettuce, cilantro. For a lot of them it is a way of saving money, and of getting money, because they sell the surplus at the farmers' market. They also sell the *sofrito*, so they do have some income from the garden. And the food definitely tastes a lot better."

Back at the office, Dan Ross, executive director of Nuestras Raices, tells me more about the connections Nuestras Raices is making in the Holyoke community.

![Jaime at La Finquita]

Jaime at La Finquita

Manuel Pantojas in a Nuestras Raices garden

![two generations of gardeners in a beanfield]

photo: Nuestras Raices

two generations of gardeners in a beanfield

Dan Ross

"Most of our members and a lot of the community members here in Holyoke grew up in rural Puerto Rico. Many came to this area as migrant workers, picking apples and tobacco. They have lifetimes of experience in agriculture. It's part of their traditions and part of their skills. The gardens are ways for them to put down roots here in the city and pass on knowledge to other generations. It's a real powerful way of bringing people together and making changes here in Holyoke."

Currently, Nuestras Raices' largest project is the Centro Agricola, still under construction. "The Centro Agricola is going to be a community education center. It will have a bilingual agricultural library, a cafe and a shared kitchen where people can have their own businesses and make their own products like *sofrito*. There's also going to be a plaza where people can gather and have parties. You can see we already have a greenhouse where we start seeds and grow bananas and other plants that like it hot." Dan says that the Centro a reflects what is unique about the organization because "it integrates a lot of different things— the restaurant with the greenhouse, space for meeting with the library."

Many of the programs sponsored by Nuestras Raices focus on community and economic development: running the farmers' market, building the Centro Agricola, and creating a market for *sofrito* and other products. But Dan makes it clear where it all started. "The heart and soul of the organization is the community gardens: all of our projects grow out of the gardens, and all of the projects are planned and implemented by the garden members. We have youth gardens in schools, and youth plots at each of our community gardens. Over 100 youth have participated in our gardening program. We have a stand at the Holyoke farmer's market and we hire our youth to work there selling produce."

Land

I ask Dan how they first got access to the land they garden, and what effect that issue has had on the gardens and the organization.

"We had enough difficulty with the city up front that all of our gardens are on private land. The owners let us use the land in exchange for paying the insurance and keeping it clean. A study at Mt. Holyoke College showed that each garden plot was growing $550 of food per season, which has helped us with the city. We calculated the total for all the five gardens and sent the report on to the mayor and other key officials.

"The real estate market in Holyoke has been bad enough that development threatening the gardens has not been a problem, but it certainly could be. We've been putting a lot of money into the Centro Agricola but as we finish with this we'll invest more money in buying our gardens and getting them into trust.

"Land ownership is key in developing community gardens; having economic development programs is crucial in establishing sustainable organizations. They allow you to reach out and create partnerships that establish a place in the community. They forge networks that help the gardens survive."

The economic development programs at Nuestras Raices reach beyond the urban plots. Dan explains that they are making connections between Holyoke and surrounding rural areas, as well as working with the many universities in the area. "We've tried to help individual members get access to farmland, loans and technical assistance when they got too big

for their little plot here. We've been working with University of Massachusetts to develop good growing techniques for crops that are traditional in Puerto Rico but have never really been grown here. We've been test-marketing certain varieties of peppers at the farmers' market to show their viability as crops in this state, and then sharing that information with farmers. We also grow them a lot in our gardens."

Beyond Nonprofit

"The way in which our organization is structured is unique," Dan continues. "We're true to our name in being grassroots. The board of directors is composed of community gardeners and other people who live right here in the community. We don't have bankers or lawyers or accountants or really rich people on our board, which would be helpful in fundraising but is less effective in terms of making the right decisions at the street level.

"The gardens elect their own board members, they write their own rules. Our projects are planned and implemented by the gardeners and by our members. Our staff don't have degrees in sustainable agriculture. We're community organizers and we're committed to helping people work together. Nuestras Raices is not really an agricultural organization. We're a community organization that's committed to building on the strengths of our community, and I think that a lot of urban agriculturalists could learn from that philosophy.

"The gardeners are proud that they're growing their own food, but most of them don't cite that as their number one reason for gardening. Most of them say how happy they are to be on the land again. They talk about being out there working with their friends, and feel a sense of tranquility being in the garden. It's important to recognize that it's not just about food. It's about building community and building connections. It isn't just agriculture, it's culture. If you recognize that you end up being more sustainable within a community because you build greater networks and you tap into a lot more resources."

The Plaza in front of the Centro Agricola is the site of many community gatherings. The landscape plan for the plaza will include varieties of Puerto Rican plants adapted to the cold Massachusetts climate. Paw-paws and hardy yellow-groove bamboo and banana (musa busjoo) will be planted around the edges of the plaza, while kiwi and passionfruit grow up the fences.

Subtropical Plants in Massachusetts

Jaime in the greenhouse at the Centro Agricola

photo: Nuestras Raices

Cultivating Communities

Joaquin Ilem Uy

an interview with Martha Goodlett

Martha Goodlett, an organic farmer and urban garden organizer, is the project coordinator for the Cultivating Communities program in Seattle, WA. We discussed her work with the organization in between bites of savory fake-meat dishes at the legendary Moonlight Cafe—a local Vietnamese restaurant and karaoke club in South Seattle.

joaquin uy: *Let's start with who you are and a description of the work you do.*

Martha Goodlett: My name is Martha Goodlett. I work for the City of Seattle Department of Neighborhoods managing a program called Cultivating Communities. It is a collaboration with the City of Seattle, the Seattle Housing Authority (SHA), and Friends of P-Patch (FPP). FPP is a non-profit corporation that works to acquire, build, preserve, and protect community gardens in Seattle neighborhoods. One of its primary missions is to break the isolation you get from living in a city, by providing opportunities for people to garden together, learn from each other, and develop a sense of neighborhood—to create a more livable urban environment. The Cultivating Communities program started in 1995. It was created to work with SHA to develop community organic gardens within their housing project communities. We receive a wide variety of funding sources: grants, contracts with SHA, donations, and produce sales from the community gardens themselves.

Gardeners with their harvest from High Point garden

Describe the community gardens.

Within the Cultivating Communities program there are three types of organic gardens. We have general community gardens, small plots for people to grow food for themselves. We have community-supported agriculture gardens. This year we have about $20,000 in produce sales from them. Seventy-five percent of those sales go directly to the gardeners; we take the other twenty-five percent to help cover the costs associated with garden upkeep. And we have youth gardens—three of them. We have a part-time staff person who holds weekly programs with kids to teach them about gardening. They love it; it's pretty exciting. In every type of garden the community members are involved in all stages of garden development, like site selection, gardener recruit-

ment, and management. We've found that this involvement and responsibility helps make the gardens active and productive.

Are the gardens concentrated in a particular area?

They're mostly concentrated in South Seattle, but we have some small gardens in the North End in courtyards of apartment buildings. We helped develop a garden in a place called Cascade Hall which serves schizophrenic residents. We don't manage the garden anymore, we just helped them get it going and provide technical assistance. They can call us at any time. We have a courtyard garden at a SHA high rise apartment building in Ballard [a north Seattle suburb]. And through Plymouth Housing, we have 2 small gardens also associated with SHA housing. But all of our bigger gardens are south.

What kind of problems in the community gardens do you receive calls about?

Well, we provide different levels of service. In most of the gardens we are the managers. We assign the plots and make sure the garden is in working order. With these gardens, the biggest challenge is maintaining up-to-date records as to who is working what plots. For instance, when someone leaves the garden—like they move or they are ill—the remaining gardeners 'colonize' the extra land without informing us of the change. It is difficult to know exactly what is going on. You can visit the garden and it will look great, and then you find out at the end of the season that some of the original gardeners are gone. Or usually what happens is someone wills their plot to the other gardeners. This is fine, but in terms of getting more people involved in the community gardens it would be good to know who is leaving so that other community members who want a plot can then get one. We want everyone to have equal access. I wouldn't call this a serious issue because at least there are no abandoned plots. But it makes it challenging to keep up with what is going on because we don't have time to make weekly visits. Fortunately, overall the gardens pretty much run themselves.

Since weekly visits are difficult, how do you handle the huge task of keeping up with the gardens?

At the beginning of each season we meet with all the gardeners and check to make sure we know 'who's on first'. We provide them with some seeds, give them organic fertilizer, and arrange for a compost delivery. We provide recycled compost once a year from Cedar Grove. We've had a bit of a problem because the compost has a residual herbicide in it called clopyralid, which doesn't break down in the Cedar Grove compost process. This makes it very difficult to grow beans, tomatoes, peas, sunflowers, and other edible plants. This has especially been a big deal in organic farming and gardening circles.

a gardener at Holly Park garden

How have the community gardens dealt with this issue of pesticides in supposedly "organic" compost?

Well, it's more than simply a matter of not using Cedar Grove compost because clopyralid is also found in a lot of hay; you then get it in manure compost too. A lot of homeowners and landscapers use it to kill off weeds. An effective way to deal with this problem would be to ban or limit the use of this herbicide. We've found that the clopyralid does eventually break down in soil after a few months; it's not like it has a half-life of a thousand years. So we are just having the gardeners mix the compost into the soil in the fall so that by the summer the pesticide is mostly broken down and not much of a harm to plants.

What are some of the challenges these urban gardens have faced in terms of protecting them from developers or even urban dwellers in the community for whom gardening isn't

so important? For instance, issues of garden security?

There is a little bit of theft, mostly of produce. It's not like we've caught anyone doing this, but there have been many reports. These have resulted in locked gardens. In the past there have been pumpkins, onions, and all kinds of produce stolen.

[Disappointedly] Most of the community gardens have locks?

MG: All of our commercial gardens have locks, because that's their livelihood. Most of our SHA gardens have locked gates too. My preference is not to have locks, but if the gardeners put in a request we'll come in and negotiate.

There's also some vandalism, which appears to be done by kids. I think they usually think of the garden as a novelty at first. They check it out, climbing fences and running through plots. And they learn that they're not supposed to be doing that. But once the garden is established, the vandalism thing usually dies down. It's not usually an ongoing problem.

Because of the collaborative nature of this program and because the land belongs to either SHA or to the organization that wants to garden, the land is very secure. However, with SHA, there has been a lot of work recently in preserving three garden projects. Three projects in Seattle have received funding to basically tear down and rebuild themselves as mixed-income communities. We have gardens in all of these communities. We are losing these gardens, but we have just been provided with funding to replace them in the new housing projects. This has been the bulk of our work for the last couple of years: rebuilding the gardens and making sure that the people in the gardens who are still in the community get their plots back.

Working the land is a way for people to be whole. It is a way for people not to be sick—whether it is physically sick or mentally sick. It helps prevent illness and helps people to get better.

How has the attitude from the community and funding organizations towards Cultivating Communities changed since its inception?

25

When the program first started out the Seattle Housing Authority was interested in having us work with them, but they didn't know exactly how. Their support was very tentative. But I would say that the program is pretty much institutionalized within the Housing Authority. Every year we are receiving contracts to continue to work with them. Though their budget is down for various reasons, they are continuing to support us. The income of the Friends of P-Patch is down this year as well, so their support is a little limited. Each city department has taken a 10-20% cut. But despite this, the Cultivating Communities program has been a high-priority program—so far.

Why do you believe it is important to have gardening communities in an urban environment?

It is a way for people to be whole. I believe this is important from personal experience and watching the gardeners—particularly immigrants who have had gardening as a part of their lives before coming to the United States. It is a way for people not to be sick—whether it is physically sick or mentally sick. It helps prevent illness and helps people to get better. When I go to the gardens and people are there working, I can feel that they are pleased with what they've grown and what they're doing. It's quite neat.

What are the demographics of the gardeners of Cultivating Communities?

Most of the gardeners involved are Southeast Asian immigrants—mainly Cambodian and Vietnamese people, and recently some Lao people. The fastest growing population of immigrants, who we are increasing outreach towards, are East African immigrants.

You mentioned the ongoing project of preserving the three gardens within the communities that are about to be demolished and rebuilt. What other projects is Cultivating Communities currently working on?

We are beginning to work more with non-profit housing groups like Southeast Senior Foundation and Mt. Baker Housing Association. There is potential to do a lot more with nonprofit housing communities because you have an instant community to work with and often these communities are very interested in gardening. We are also focusing on doing outreach with particular populations. For instance, we don't have very many African-Americans involved in our P-Patch Programs. So we have a VISTA volunteer going out to community meeting places for African Americans such as churches, neighborhood association meetings to see if there is interest in community gardeners. This is also

true for Latino populations; we don't have very many members of this group involved.

What is your long term vision for Cultivating Communities?

The city council has adopted a 'five-year plan' for the P-Patch Program. The Friends of P-Patch is a part of it. The plan is to add 5 gardens a year in the city with a focus on low-income communities and for low-income people. So far, we are meeting our goals. However, we aren't getting new staff and we're not going to be getting new staff. If anything, we're going to see cuts. So you have all the old gardens and then you add 5 new ones a year, with no new staff. A dilution of service results. So we're going through a debate as to whether it is more important to add new gardens or well-manage the existing ones. My feeling is let's just build gardens and people can adapt to taking care of them. They may not be run exactly like you want them to be, but at least there are gardens and people to take care of them.

Cultivating Communities & housing projects

I agree with this strategy. I am an action-oriented individual. There is so much potential space out there to be utilized for such endeavors. For instance, in the neighborhood I live in, there are at least two huge empty lots nearby; mostly of dirt piles and weeds. They would be perfect for a community garden.

Me too. I feel like it just makes sense to go into the South End and try to buy up a bunch of land for gardens because in 10 or 15 years it's going to be extremely densely populated. Now is the time—when the land is relatively cheap.

Currently, the P-Patch strategy is to put up gardens in areas that are already very densely populated. But, the reality is that there are not a lot of places open. So say, "Okay, let's instead do something down South and get prepared for the future."

Do you have any further thoughts about your organization?

When I came on there were different people who wanted to intern or volunteer. At first I discouraged it because I didn't know what I was doing or what was going on. But now internships seem like a really great thing. We've had interns from Evergreen College and from Iowa, as well as other places. It is really important to expose as many people to information about gardening organically and cross-cultural gardening. It is important to be able to understand and get along with people from different places in the world.

Out of the Rubble

text and photos by Sol Kinnis

In search of the great agricultural oasis of the revolutionary Cuban cities, I headed south on a three month contract to research urban agriculture in Cuba. It has become well known among many urban gardening activists that Cuba is miles ahead of most in feeding its urban citizens out of their own backyards. My experiences of urban agriculture in Havana spanned a short period of time, during which I was more absorbed by living in a place so unlike anywhere I'd been before—a little nation that tries so hard to do unlike anywhere else in the world— than I was in gardens. But I was there long enough to understand that what makes urban agriculture in Havana so unique is that everyone is in it together— backyard gardeners, farmers, doctors, artists, musicians, cooks, researchers, journalists, social workers, to name just a few. I haven't quite pieced it all together yet, but I'd like to share some of my observations and to pass on a few stories from my Cuban friends and colleagues.

Hunger

In 1987 my friend was in Angola as part of his two year military service, his first time away from his Cuban homeland. He was struck by the sight of stray dogs wandering the streets of Luanda; this was something he never saw back home in Cuba. But he returned home at the end of his service, just after the USSR collapsed, to find dogs starving and dragging their skin behind them. But of course it wasn't just the dogs going hungry. He and many others told me first hand accounts of what it was like never having enough to eat, the difficulty of getting from one place to the next with no personal energy and no public transportation.

A big question for many North Americans concerned with local food security issues is what would happen if we were cut off from the global food chain. How would we survive when such a small percentage of our food is produced locally? As a result of the collapse of the Soviet Union, Cuba was forced to contend with this question. Prior to 1989, Cuba was dependent on the USSR for over 85% its trade, including agricultural equipment, pesticides, fertilizers, and fuel for transportation. The sudden loss of this trade resulted in a massive food crisis that was dealt with immediately through extreme rationing, marking the beginning of what is called the Special Period. To survive in the long term, a major transformation of agricultural production in the country was required.

Almost overnight, Cuba began making the transition from high input, state-run industrial agriculture to low input, decentralized organic agriculture. To set an example for what needed to be done, the Ministry of Agriculture even dug up its front lawn and planted vegetables. Urban agriculture quickly became a vital part of the urban food chain. Twelve years later the movement for urban sustainability continues.

Activism

Down a gravel road from my home in Central

In Old Havana, the narrow streets and old dense buildings leave little space for gardening. As the buildings collapse, many of the empty lots are made available to urban farmers.

Havana, riding through holes filled by water from the broken water lines of this old colonial city, I find my way to the metal gate to the well-known patio of Justo Torres. I pass through the unlocked bars, and am welcomed by my co-workers. I have caught the attention of the young school children, here to visit this inner city garden. I park my bike against a Guanabana tree, a now rare sweet and sour fruit indigenous to Cuba, and make my way past the kids, busy writing in their notebooks and listening to Justo talk passionately about urban gardening. This day is Justo's birthday, and to celebrate the occasion, Cuban singer-songwriter Theresita Fernandez entertains the group with her songs that celebrate nature and their Cuban homeland.

Justo Torres is a well known and respected community permaculture advocate, practitioner and educator. Justo is an activist I can relate to. He's creating alternatives. He's inspired with a vision for change and he's doing it. He's here to stay and is willing to do the work. In only three years, his patio has set an example for neighbors and inner-city gardeners of how to grow a highly productive and diverse garden in a tiny space. Using urban permaculture techniques, Justo grows over 50 species of vegetables, fruits, *viandas* (root crops), medicinal herbs and ornamental plants, that help to supplement the diets of his family, friends and neighbors.

My job over the next three months would be to work with Justo and to interview gardeners in Cerro, a large municipality, bordering on Old Havana and Central Havana, who are participating in the 'Patio Project', a project designed to provide the education and support needed to grow food in any spaces available in their urban neighborhoods.

Justo points to a *Zunzun*, a once-rare hummingbird that has come to feed on the flower of the giant banana tree that grows out of his compost pile. He tells me that since he developed the patio, he has noticed numerous species of birds and insects that he had never seen in his neighborhood before. They have come to feed on the diversity of flowers and fruits his garden has to offer. At the back of the patio, he raises guinea pigs which he promotes as a highly nutritious and easy-to-care-for source of protein.

The patio of Justo Torres is home to over 50 plant species and several guinea pigs.

Food

Everyone asks me if people in Cuba have enough to eat. As in all parts of the world the answer is "Well, that depends." In Cuba that depends on finances, where you live and what's available.

In North America, in my experience, housing is the basic necessity that takes up most of our monthly income. Food usually comes in a far second. In Cuba it is food that consumes most of the monthly income. For many people, in fact, food is

In North America housing is the basic necessity that takes up most of our monthly income. Food usually comes in a far second. In Cuba, for many people, food is the only expenditure, and often monthly income isn't enough to feed the family.

the only expenditure and often the monthly income isn't even enough to feed the family. This despite the *libreta*. The *libreta* is the food rations book given to each household which guarantees every family a daily loaf of bread and a certain portion of meat, rice, beans, roots, vegetables and fruits, as available. This ration accounts for, I'm told, about 60% of an average house-

28

hold's dietary needs. The remainder comes from people's salaries or other income sources. Fresh vegetables, when available, are particularly expensive in relation to people's income.

I would often meet up with Justo at his place and we would walk or bike to one of the gardener's places that he would want me to interview. One day he took me to meet an older couple, probably in their 80s. They live in a small house, one of a row of houses, much like a one-level townhouse complex, stretching back from the road. Their door opens onto a once-empty lot. (The original building on this lot collapsed.) Now the land has been subdivided into small patios, each about 16 square meters, one for each of the complex residents. All had developed their patio into a food garden in their own way. The couple I met had two fruit trees, some vegetable beds and a couple of chickens.

They told me how thankful they were that Justo had helped them to develop their garden. Before they hadn't had enough to eat. Their old age pension, provided in *pesos*, was no longer enough to live on, as basic necessities such as eggs were only available to them in dollars. Their garden provided them with at least part of what they weren't able to access in the market. They said that whatever they couldn't eat they would share with family and neighbors. I couldn't quite understand how they were able to share when their garden seemed so sparse. After I

Esperanza is a woman who raises Melipona bees, indigenous to Cuba, on her rooftop. The view from her rooftop overlooks the municipality of Cerro.

Many people raise animals on their patios or rooftops, including chickens, pigs, guinea pigs, rabbits, ducks and even one farmer who has a herd of goats.

At a day-care in Cerro old hydroponics structures are filled with compost and used for intensive gardening.

spent the day with them, they gave me an egg. Their two chickens provided them with one to two eggs per day.

Land

Resources such as fuel, soil, water, gardening tools and seeds are scarce in the inner-city of Havana. So is land. Some of the people I met in Cerro are growing food on their rooftops, but for a large percentage of inner city Havana residents, this is not an option.

Many of the buildings in the older parts of Havana are centuries old. Worn away by hurricanes and age, with few resources to restore them, these buildings are collapsing and forcing residents to move. And many of those structures that haven't yet fallen are not secure enough to hold up a rooftop garden.

Fortunately, land distribution is a non-profit system, and when land is not being used, it is often made accessible to meet the direct needs of the community.

Today I am interviewing Raúl, a retired poet and patio gardener. Rather than talk of vegetables, he prefers to discuss poetry, and the color of my eyes. I steer him on to politics. He gives me a little lesson in local Cuban governmental structure. In the cities, each municipality is divided into consejos (or what would be roughly equivalent to our 'neighborhoods'). The *consejo popular* is the neighborhood level government, recognized by the municipality as having limited governing power over the

Medicine

At a meeting to discuss a new permaculture education center in Old Havana, a doctor spoke about his work in mapping out all of the medicinal plants in the neighborhood.

With the ongoing US embargo against Cuba, western medicines are difficult to obtain. Doctors rely on green medicines for a significant amount of their treatments, and local sources of herbs are not taken for granted. During my visit to a

Raúl is proud of his small patio garden where he uses all kinds of containers to grow vegetables for himself and his neighbors.

neighborhood. Their meetings include representatives from neighborhood organizations such as schools, clinics, and cultural groups, where they address issues such as how to provide activities for youth, increasing the availability of food and medicine in the neighborhood, and developments on vacant land.

Each *consejo* is further divided into circumscriptions which are themselves divided into CDR's, the Cuban Spanish acronym for Revolutionary Defense Committees. Each CDR represents approximately 20 to 40 households and were originally formed as a military strategy to defend and promote the revolution at the grassroots. Today CDR's are responsible for block level issues. For example, if you want to garden on an empty lot where a building has fallen down, you would first approach the CDR to see if there are any other plans for that land, and to discuss what the residents think about a garden being developed there. If the idea is welcomed, you get the land. I was also told that CDR's are responsible for maintaining discipline on the block, but that's another article.

At the geriatrics hospital in Cerro, patients and staff have developed a permaculture plan for their building and the land around it. From left to right are the director of the hospital, Justo Torres, head gardener/patient, and a doctor.

herb farm, developed on the empty lot where a building once stood in the inner-city municipality of Vedado, I spoke with the farm coordinator about the connection of local herb farmers with local doctors. He explained that they work closely with the neighborhood health representative to find out what herbs are needed for health concerns in the area and so that the doctors know what is available. Doctors need to know what is available in order to write prescriptions for their patients.

A group of patients at the geriatrics hospital in Cerro have taken this a step further. In a permaculture course led by Justo, they created a permaculture design for their hospital which includes growing both food and medicine to be used to meet the needs of the many eld-

A medicinal herb garden where farmers make use of whatever materials are available for building garden beds.

erly patients. They have the full support of the doctors and the director of the hospital who proudly detailed their collective vision and the potential benefits that their garden will bring to the patients. The head gardener is an enthusiastic patient at the hospital. He took the afternoon to tell me about how good he felt to be growing food as he led me on a tour around the current and future garden at the hospital.

Most of the activists I meet talk about their work as cultural work, that of creating a culture of nature, where nature equals trees equals food equals medicine.

Culture

What inspired me most about the permaculture movement in Havana was that despite its early stage of development, people from a wide range of disciplines are coming together to implement their new ideas. They understand the need to connect issues in order to

Banana trees are a fast and easy way to get fruit in Cuba.

meet people's needs. In Cuba, the environment means everything, not just trees. It means trees and medicine and food and people and houses as well.

Havana's permaculture activists are meeting to develop a joint permaculture project with the Cuban Botanical

Society. They're thinking big. They plan to work at a neighborhood level throughout the city to support the creation of permaculture gardens. Additional plans include hosting cultural activities to promote environmental education, developing information centers, hosting permaculture workshops and promoting diets high in locally grown produce.

Most of the activists I meet talk about their work as cultural work, that of creating a culture of nature, where nature equals trees equals food equals medicine.

There are only two channels on TV, both government owned and commercial free, and while they may be, as many people suggest, instruments of government propaganda, there appears to be space for local messages that reach many people. When I told my host family about this couple that I met who do workshops on canning, they said "Oh yeah, I used to watch their cooking show." When I mention Fundación, most people have heard about it because they have seen my co-workers interviewed on TV or they've heard organizers talking on the radio about their permaculture workshops. For a city of two million people, Havana felt like a small town. The media's focus on what Cubans are doing to defend the revolution (which includes everything from military service to urban gardening) contributes to this small town feeling.

I'm sitting with my friends in the Casa de Musica, finishing the last of our rum and colas. As the music ends, the lights come on and the waiters begin to clear the tables. My friend and dance instructor Julio sits in the chair beside me. A small group of men, artists, musicians and intellectuals have joined us. They are captivated by Julio's tale: not of love or war or community gossip, but of the banana tree growing out of the garbage heap in one of Havana city's community gardens. "On cement?" someone asks.

With a foot of compost made from food scraps, they had grown one of the biggest banana trees Julio had ever seen, right here in the city. Everyone in the group is amazed by this miracle.

Urban Farms

IN THE FIELDS AND IN THE STREETS
RESIST
CORPORATE CONTROL OF SUSTENANC

Saskatchewan, Canada • Detroit, MI • Seattle, WA • Tacoma, WA • Tucson, AZ

"I'm looking at urban agriculture as a way to undermine the industrial agriculture system—the way that global food production works."

—Jess Hayes

To farm in the city is to move both backwards and forwards in time. A hundred fifty years ago, major cities had farms on the outskirts, and city dwellers expected fresh milk delivered daily. Cows grazed the Boston Common, while in many western cities urbanization and small truck farms hung in a quickly disappearing balance.

Industry attracted more and more people to cities, paving and building on formerly cultivated land. But it was the industrialization of agriculture that made small farms unprofitable, shifting most people's food source to large, distant chemical-dependent farms.

During World War II, vacant urban land was used for Victory Gardens—New York's Tompkin's Square Park was divided into garden plots. Many recent arrivals from rural areas easily adapted their gardening skills to an urban setting, only to replace the food gardens with grass and pavement after the war was over.

As aquifers are depleted and agricultural soils collapse, city dwellers may be forced to take responsibility for growing their food regionally once again. If urban farmers like those in Boston and Detroit have their way, the vast tracts of land made available by burning in the 1970s and the flight of industry will one day be productive farms that contribute significantly to urban food security.

Jessica Hayes, who worked with The Food Project on environmental justice in Boston, MA has a vision of how to begin this transformation.

"I'm looking at urban agriculture as a way to undermine the industrial agriculture system—the way that global food production works." she says. "I can fight that system until I die, but at the same time build an alternative so at some point we can just cut the global system off. By working on a local level with the support of local policy makers, getting people in the Dudley neighborhood to be more of a voice about backyard gardeners and environmental justice issues, we can have an impact.

"Let's be really idealistic for a second and say that we were able to do large-scale food production in Boston—that would really change people's relationship to immediate pollution. Right now people have the idea that they're so removed from food pollution, pesticides, the spraying for the West Nile Virus, because they come into the supermarket and buy food off the shelf. It would be amazing to see what would happen as far as people's demand for cleaner air and cleaner water if they saw the food they eat growing in their neighborhoods. Local food production would have an impact on the broader environment as well, by taking the pressure of industrial food production off of rural and wild lands. We could become less dependent on the transportation networks, on fossil fuels, on irrigation and water infrastructure. Agriculture wraps them all together."

Down on the Canadian Industrial Farm

Andrea del Moral

Saskatchewan, Canada

While living in Montréal in 1999, I got involved in anti-genetic engineering resistance. My friends and I had a big papier mâché tomato fish and we held parades through town, made up theatre about mad science, arranged a public debate about the ethics of biotechnology, and held the first supermarket protest in the city. We knew we were just city kids though, and we touched the food system only as Consumers. We didn't like the spin of the corporate media and we didn't trust it. The genetically engineered crops we heard about were far outside the city. We decided we had to go to the fields where they were being grown. We had to seek out the stories of people living amongst this technology, people who were using it, opposing it, keeping quiet or doing something about it. Three friends and I embarked on a trip across Canada in the harvest season—August and September, 1999. We found a world that touched each of us deeply, that motivates us daily to innovate a better relationship to food and the land. Sometimes I cry remembering this trip and the huge complexity of the problems people talked to us about. Other times I feel like we'll soon be changing the world in significant ways because there are people all over this land striving for the same thing. When our work and their work meets up, we're going to find we've created the world we're dreaming about and building today.

The journey starts with a seed. An idea, a hope, capable of anything once it catches wind and goes—somewhere, anywhere, a thousand wheres. We were traveling hard, passing fast, putting several hundred miles and dozens of towns behind us, jammed into one blink of memory each. Between them, corn filled the space. Acres and acres of corn that went on forever. The heartland? This corn does not feed people. It's made into carcinogenic ethanol (a gasoline additive), animal feed, and high fructose corn syrup for junk food that takes the place of whole grains and fresh vegetables in entire neighborhoods back in the city. From the highway, tall stalks heavy with drying ears blur together into an idyllic landscape. Some people come out here to escape the city but the human in us smears this land with fingerprints—cylindrical silos cluster on each end of the horizon, and a lone machine creeps through a field.

We're standing under a grain silo on an 8000 acre farm in Ontario that works drying the beans and grains 24 hours a day. Looking up we see the steel infrastructure crisscross against the horizon, against the grain, against the contours of land. The brain behind this job sits in that box on the wall, directs the machinery around us constantly, then phones home when the beans are dry. The sound rings through in the only house in sight—and how many bodies work this 8000 acre farm? Five.

Marty Pavel is one of them. "Been farming my whole life," he says. Except for thirteen years in the railroad car factory, cuz "I was a good farmer, but nobody taught me finance." When Marty couldn't pay even the interest on his loans, the bank took his land and sold it cheap to more financially promising farmers. The Van Osch's bought Marty's farm and later hired him back to manage livestock. "Farming

top: a cornfield in Saskatchewan

bottom left: a canola seedpod contaminated with genetically engineered pollen from a nearby crop of Roundup-Ready seed.

center: silos drying the harvest

top right: the brain behind the machines

bottom right: chemical inputs such as Lact-a-Fat have become essential to the health of cows crowded into feedlots.

big is the way of the future. The small guy can still live—he's just gotta have work outside it." Fifty years ago, when Marty's parents were farming, a family could make a living with 50 sows. Now, 300 won't keep you. Of course, 100 years ago, 80% of folks were farmers and they had more political influence and say in their survival. Now less than 3% of the population farms "for a living," and thousands less are able to do it every year.

Marty's parents farmed with horses, grew mixed grains, had a large family. Now, feeding the cows is a full-time job. Vitamin E so the meat is redder, Lact-a-Fat byproduct for the precise dietary balance, a micromanaged feed lot with a manure sludge trench out the back, everything carefully designed so that in a year's time, the cows will make it off this lot worth a dollar or two profit per head. "I work 70, 80, 90 hours a week, 7 days. Year round. In the spring and fall my son works 100 or more a week. This isn't a solution; it's a matter of living. Survival."

We gather these stories, that the unheroic efforts to save a livelihood will not be forgotten. We come from the cities, at least one generation away from all this, but we're the spiritual children of these dwellers on the land, troubadours, come to gather songs of desperate hope. We're angry, embittered, livid that these crimes remain invisible. There are big spaces to think about these things. This feeling expands until halted by icons of the city; grain silos, shiny silver flashes in the early autumn sun seem as alien as spaceships landing in crop circles. The granaries are all named POOL—supposedly cooperatives but only in name and membership fee.

Industrial Farms, Industrial Cities

These farmers are the hardest working, most underpaid members of society, and every single person depends on them daily but doesn't really know what that means. How did it happen that this is what living on a farm meant? It wasn't always this way. We stay with people whose families have farmed the same land since the 1860s. Back then, Clare's grandfather built yellow bricks from the mud, grew food for the family and animals, as well as for export to the cities further east. It was back-breaking work, cold lonely work. No romantic life. The governments of Canada

and the US made it easy to get land to live on; they were funding railroad expansion and needed farmers to provide food for the booming industrialization of Toronto, Pittsburgh and New York City. They were trying to populate the wild "unpopulated" Indian country, with European blood. They were building an urban-rural industrial system in which hardworking poor in both places produced wares for corporations who controlled the transfer and sale between these distant markets. And it worked.

Instead of dumping this chemical on "the enemy," the government now dumped it into food fields of their own people. The whole idea behind chemicals pesticides, herbicides and fertilizers was that you could grow more food for less money, less labor, less crop failure, on less land.

Once farmers had staked out the land, the government changed the pace. The falling price of food meant farmers tried to grow more just to maintain the same farm income. At the end of World War II, men returning home headed to the cities. They hungered for the cosmopolitan life, having seen some of the world. The farms had managed with fewer hands during the war year, and new machines meant that even fewer people needed to work the land. Many veterans went to cities and suburbs, where lots of jobs were available in industry. Industrial expansion took off because the energy toward the war was suddenly freed up for production. While steel and electrical industries refocused toward automobiles, refrigerators, and housing developments—the gadgets of suburban lifestyle—the chemical manufacturers looked for a new application for their nitrogen technology which had been used for making bombs.

billboard in Saskatchewan

Instead of dumping this chemical on "the enemy," the government now dumped it into food fields of their own people. The whole idea behind chemicals pesticides, herbicides and fertilizers was that you could grow more food for less money, less labor, less crop failure, on less land. It wasn't that most farmers were trying to get rich. They were trying to survive. But with each year that farmers bought chemicals and machines, their self-reliance slipped a little further. A cycle of connection

All this open space lets you breathe large, but at the end of that breath, the heavy history weighs in, and the largeness of space feels too much to bear. The neighbor farmer is the Novartis sales rep, another sells the John Deere equipment. The company's roots are sunk deep into the community. Your neighbor needs it to pay the mortgage, you need it to harvest your crops, to pay the mortgage on the expensive machines you need...to harvest the crops again. This is how it's done here now.

Percy and the Invasion of the Seed

Roundup, made by Monsanto corp, is the best-selling garden pesticide in the world. In the mid-1990's, Monsanto released a new "Roundup-Ready" seed line into its soy, canola, corn and cotton markets. "Roundup-Ready" technology is a genetic modification that allows crops to survive higher applications of this toxic herbicide—thus promoting ever-increasing profits for Monsanto and increasing farmers' chemical dependence.

Like most agricultural biotechnology companies, Monsanto requires farmers to sign a contract when they buy genetically engineered seed. This agreement, which prohibits farmers from saving seed for next year's planting, or sharing, trading or selling the seed also allows Monsanto to hire private investigators to inspect customers' fields for years after they purchase seed. These inspectors also typically inspect non-customer's fields and in 1998 sued Percy Schmeiser for patent infringement.

Percy Schmeiser with contaminated canola

Percy Schmeiser

I have two miles of land where there's a power line going alongside the edge. It's not very far into the land so we can't cultivate in between the powerlines and the road. If you keep the rest of your land clean, you'll have the weeds growing around the power pole—so we spray that by hand, using Roundup." Percy Schmeiser is a 60-some-odd field crop (canola, wheat, rye, corn) farmer in Bruno, Saskatchewan. He's been growing canola for over 40 years, and saving the best of it to grow again the next year—a personal breeding project, so that his canola will do better in the conditions of his field.

In 1997 we noticed that after we were through spraying around the power poles, about 60% of the canola didn't die. I knew something was wrong. Having grown canola for many years, I thought maybe we'd mixed the chemical wrong. We waited about a week and then I went out and took the sprayer, made sure it had the right formula, and sprayed it again. We waited about a week. It killed canola but a lot of it was still alive. As you got further into the field, more of it got killed. I realized that my canola had developed resistance to the Roundup, or something was different in my seed.

In 1998 I used seed from 1997, and apparently somebody realized, or I might have even mentioned, that my canola

didn't die around the poles, and all of a sudden I got a lawsuit launched against me from Monsanto. Up to that point I'd never had anything to do with Monsanto. I was using my own seed and I firmly believe now that I got to some extent a Roundup-Ready canola in about 900 acres of land, which I don't want.

There is a former Monsanto employee in the area, he's an ex-RCMP, he works for Robinson Investigation. All these people that Monsanto has hired when farmers get informed on by their neighbors, Robinson Investigation are the people that they hire. They'll go try to get samples from your crop, without permission, take canola. If I was to go to St. Louis, Missouri and went into their laboratories and took plants or papers, you know where I would end up. They think they're so big, god, and all mighty that they can do anything and nobody's going to stand up to them. In my case, I never had anything to do with Monsanto before. So if they can do that to me, what's stopping them from doing that to anybody else? I was using my own seed from one year to another. They want to stop that.

They want to have it so that farmers always have to go and buy seed. If they can control the seed supply, they can control the food supply, and if you control the food supply, you control the nation. Or the world.

Percy Schmeiser was forced to pay $105,000 in damages to Monsanto. He is suing Monsanto for libel, trespass and contamination of his fields with Roundup Ready canola.

to the land was broken, and farms were connected to machines, chemicals, and the market economy.

Successful "farmers" are more accurately good machinists, mechanics and accountants. They like working without a boss and getting outside sometimes. But their rhythms run on the gas gauge, not the sun's pace. Farmers need money more than before just to keep the farm running, so they grow things based on what pays the bills instead of what people need and want. The inertia of this system is inevitable. It's taken a few

decades to become obvious, but even city folk can see what's happening.

People of the land are a rare breed and dwindling. Each year more and more who were just scraping by get blown off the land. They move on to city rhythms and small towns, unforgiven by the land they rolled over in steel tractors, compacting the earth with tall wheels and deafened to its music by loud engines, 18, 20 hours a day during the harvest. But it's either work for the man or work for the man, and it's less painful sometimes if you don't have to watch the soil spirits die beneath tractor wheels and pesticide meals. That's all that's been said out here. If you want to keep the house, eat next winter or be at all efficient, you're going to want a bigger farm. The city folk want big cheap supermarkets to be stocked and if you don't do it, Mr. and Ms. Farmer, there are global trade policies that will make you regret it.

Free Markets or a Free World?

All of the trade agreements in effect in the world right now are about removing what free trade supporters call "trade barriers." From the perspective of farmers, "trade barriers" are support structures that help them survive against the global "free" market. Except for the corporate farms and processing plants, removing these social systems is like letting a fox into the chicken coop. That fence is a very good idea if you are not equipped to compete. Some people say that if you can't compete, you should go out of business and work for someone more efficient. Well, in the year 2000, 20,000 of the 200,000 farmers in the Canadian prairies were forced out of farming. In one year, ten percent of farmers were too 'inefficient' to deserve to stay in farming.

The summer before the Seattle ministerial, the US Department of Agriculture made a propaganda packet about how the World Trade Organization (WTO) is good for the US. The USDA packet admits that "a more liberal world trading system in agricultural products benefits the US more than any other country." But who is meant by the "US" here? "Free trade" benefits large, established companies, because a level playing field is great if you're bigger than everyone else. Farmers aren't doing any better. People aren't eating any better. A couple of corporations are getting richer in the name of "the US" and at the expense of people and ecosystems everywhere. The foxes in the chicken coop don't like the chickens to raise fences to protect themselves, but it's the foxes, not the people of the US who benefit from this "free" market mania.

At the FTAA meeting in April 2001, the US Trade Representative pushed to leave food—like all other products—to the whims of the economy and the men who make its rules. Who are these men? The powerful lobbies that dictate a corporate agenda—the Dairy Association, the Biotechnology Industry Organization, the American Corn Growers Association. So of course the people's "representatives" in congress wind up with two priorities when they make food policy: keep the government rolling in dough and keep corporations happy. As these food policies take effect, people in the cities are left eating overprocessed food with no nutri-

tion, and kids grow up malnourished, addicted to sugar and dependent on food stamps. Distributors and processors make money while farmers lose their land, and people everywhere starve for healthy food.

In cities and the country, the means of survival slip from people's grip, but the economy continues on its "logical" progression— and it is always "making progress."

The goal of our agricultural system is no longer to feed ourselves and one another. It's a profit system, not a food system.

The corporations are coming on strong, yet the farmers can't tell you exactly what's wrong—so they keep their mouths shut, don't talk about bum deals with the biotech barons who're invading their fields, cuz they might come after you next time. The toll-free rat-on-your-neighbor hotline for illegally, unwittingly having genetically-engineered seed turns these towns into breeding grounds for hatred and fear. This is a complicated land of integrity and compromise, hard work and kind eyes.

This is the heartland of the empire. But even the seemingly greatest of empires falls to something...but what? No one can afford to even work the land in the grips of the market's ruthless hands. Chased out by the need to survive, these are the lives they've left behind: abandoned roadside cafés and towns of aging farmers, the kids run off to the cities, or to more dependable work. All this open space lets you breathe large, but at the end

In the city and in the country, the same thing is happening to us all—we're being dispossessed of the land. Closed in by concrete, steel, and gasoline, broken from the rhythms of the seasons and the soil, we've got our work to do, too.

of that breath, the heavy history weighs in, and the largeness of space feels too much to bear. Clarity of the situation is lacking. The neighbor farmer is the Novartis sales rep, another sells the John Deere equipment. The company's roots are sunk deep into the community. Your neighbor needs it to pay the mortgage, you need it to harvest your crops, to pay the mortgage on the expensive machines you need...to harvest the crops again. This is how it's done here now.

The Way Out

We know this isn't the only way to feed each other. But the people who grow this food don't share our hope. Marty tells us, "Food won't be priced accurately or justly. Cuz they'll just get it from another country. So we have to get smarter. We'd prefer to be self-sufficient, no depending on another country. But the United States is boss. Period. They tell us what to do." This is not just the story of Canada. America, we too have this problem. It's not the United States that's boss—it's a system of elites. The people out here and back in the city are waiting for—something. Someone. Some solution to jump out of the sky to change this. But miracles don't happen on their own. They take soulfuls of passion, a spark of ingenuity, and a lifelong armful of dedication.

For a long time now we've been asking: how do we find a way out of this? On the surface, city landscapes look so different from the expanses of grain and beans that stretch through the middle of the continent. But just as the monoculture of plants is not grown to feed people, neither is the space in cities dedicated to meeting the daily needs of the people who live there.

In the city and in the country, the same thing is happening to us all—we're being dispossessed of the land. Closed in by concrete, steel, and gasoline, broken from the rhythms of the seasons and the soil, we've got our work to do, too. As city folk we've got a responsibility to reclaim that connection. So do we bring plants to the city, in any form possible? Streetcorner corn plots won't feed San Francisco, but maybe we're on to something. Concrete doesn't have to be the final layer. Bringing our real selves up to the surface, our histories, our desires, making our future from the past, not the sudden corporate concrete cast, not the paralyzing current clash—these will not last. Out of the supermarket's fluorescent glare, a hand-cared for farm is there and every year sweet rewards come to those whose tools are shovels and fingernails stained with dirt. They yield harvests of plant varieties that Safeway denies you and Whole Foods is scared to surprise you with. Cuz it's hard to be interesting when growing food by machine—low tech means bring on the beans with scarecrow goddesses and kings of the field.

In Saskatchewan, the fields run a quarter-mile square. In the city I live in, the biggest open space is a commuter park & ride parking lot. So we start with what we got. Our fields aren't big enough to engulf tractors, or funnel up into the bypass-the-people global food highway, but this is not how solutions are made anyway. Finding a way out will require a hard look at the roots of these problems and discovering ways different people are trying to solve them. We can create our own potential solutions each day we touch and listen to the land. We need to do it together, because working in a garden alone doesn't heal the isolation, the alienation, and the disempowerment that monocultures breed.

Change comes from empowerment, and power comes from people putting their capabilities, their stories, their strength and support together. When we open ourselves up to each other, the power to act on our desires becomes a possibility—and this is what we're after: the power not just to have dreams but to create those dreams in the world. I say "we" and I think of people in rural Ontario, Saskatchewan, and Oregon, I think of city folk in Oakland, Tacoma, Montréal—it's a bigger "we" than any one of us will ever meet. Amongst us, we have the ideas that could change this mess into good food and free lives. That begins with knowing and trusting each other, working with the people around us.

Beginners

Darryl, an organic mixed-grain farmer in Radisson, Saskatchewan tells us, "Somehow we have to be involved in food production other than just growing the stuff and handing it over to somebody to take away. Because in conventional agriculture, traditionally farmers have not maintained any control or involvement in what happens to their products. If organic agriculture does that, we'll be exploited and we'll find ourselves in exactly the same boat."

It's interesting, this fox and chicken idea. The foxes need the chickens, but the chickens don't need the foxes. Of course any time we try to create our own lives, they're going to try to stop us, tell us we don't know what we're doing, can't do it, are hurting other people. Sometimes we're gullible and believe it.

We're city folk, not experts at feeding each other or solving these insidious problems. But this is exactly the point. "Last year," Darryl says, "was my 25th crop and I still don't really consider myself a farmer. If I'd had some basic education in agriculture I might have been hindered much more by convention than I am now. But when I go out to decide what I'm growing and how to plant it, I'm a beginner." This is where we all start: willing to be beginners. Taking a chance, we can shape our own circumstance. So that when spring comes around, there's a piece of earth nearby where we can come together with other people, dig our hands in, and begin to plant another seed. Knowing that we are the only ones who can make the worlds we desire—and that we have the power to make seeds grow.

Casa del Sol, Bronx, NY

photo by Jeff Conant

Farming in the Motor City

interviews with Grace Boggs and Jim Stone

Grace Boggs

Farm-a-lot

Under the Coleman Young [Detroit Mayor, mid-1970s] administration the Farm-a-Lot program was created. The program gives out seeds in the spring to people, and helps with the tilling of the land. There is some recognition here in Detroit that the land has not been as valuable here as it has been in, say, New York. Even in New York, there are 500 community gardens. I just came back from New York, and they have ten thousand vacant lots there, and only five hundred community gardens. You'd be hard-pressed to find the vacant lots, though.

Here you see them all over. There's been some concern about the use of these lots, because they're not owned by the people who garden them. Still, unless they're in the particular areas that the developers want, they're not likely to be taken away. Most of the thousands of lots are city-owned.

Jim Stone

In Detroit we've got all kinds of vacant land: the supply and demand issues make it pretty easy to get land to farm on. There's so much vacant land in the city, and once the weeds get high the Recreation Department doesn't have the budget to mow on a regular basis. So it's to the city's advantage to have someone maintaining the land by growing food on it, and they encourage it. You apply to the city through the Recreation Department. The ideal situation is to get permission from the landowner. The city has a one-sheet contract that's really easy to fill out.

Farming a Baseball Field

The city-owned vacant land next to the Katherine Fergueson Academy is our six acres and a mule. Farmer Paul (Paul Weertz) takes the tractor over. He's got a hay baler. It's the coolest thing in the world. I'm not

Six acres of urban oats recently cut for hay

sure the field's actually six acres, but it's a big chunk, planted in hay and alfalfa. Katherine Fergueson Academy is an old elementary school that was converted into a high school for nursing and pregnant mothers. They had a baseball field and backstops, and they hadn't had a pickup baseball game there in years.

The first year we disked the land. We had the alternative workforce there, my pickup truck with the flatbed trailer, and some shovels. Mrs. Perry down at the soup kitchen organized some of the seniors to cook. We hit up the food stores for some guilt money, and they

photos by Chris Stein

Inter-generational exchange in a Detroit Agricultural Network garden

40

donated some ribs, hot dogs, hamburgers and chickens and we had a big old barbecue. We got out some greens, and just had a party. We said to the folks from the jail, "Take the goddamn orange vests off." We knew the parole officers, and they understood our approach. The guys were so grateful. Someone still had to stand there with a gun and a radio in case someone was going to run. Everybody was cool. They did all the hard grunt work, and Farmer Paul started growing the hay and alfalfa after disking all the weeds under. It's been three years now, and he cuts it two or three times a year as a cash crop. He uses it as feed for the animals, and trucks some down to the county fair to sell.

Farmer Paul keeps goats, chickens, rabbits and a small horse on the school. They got a variance from the city. The city wanted them to put the animals outside the city limits, but it's educational, so they let them stay. Any schools that have land of any kind are a good candidate for gardens, especially if the land's not utilized.

After we disked and plowed and got all the gunk out, phase two was to get the landscapers to dump all their shredded leaves and lawn clippings, and we got some soil amendments. They got a grant for fruit trees, and planted them on the perimeter. Paul converted an outbuilding, and got the chickens and the rabbits and the horse. The old ball field was planted with hay and alfalfa. They put in pumpkins and cash crops— stuff that the students could deal with. He took some land that was a bunch of weeds, and made it productive.

"Bad Guys": Farming Urban Soil

Farming in the city is a lot of work. We soil test everything, and in general it's not as bad as we'd expected. We've tested some real nasty sites for lead, cadmium and volatile organic compounds—all the bad guys. They were found, but not any more than the ambient level across the region. But we play it safe. When we disk and plant, we put compost around the row where the plant is. Every year we keep building up that base.

On some sites we've gone with raised beds, because we want to assure people that the food is as safe and as clean as you can get. People think we're crazy to farm such an industrialized area, but people living here have the right to fresh food, and it makes

top: Farmer Paul's tractor in an urban peach orchard
middle: goats at the school eating urban hay
bottom: an abandoned house is used as a haybarn to store 250 bales

41

more sense to grow it right here than to truck it in from all over the country.

The Detroit Agricultural Network

Grace Boggs

Gerald [Hairston] is really a gardener, his whole heart is in gardening. He'd been doing a lot of gardening with a number of people in the neighborhood who we call the Gardening Angels, who are mostly elders. This was ten years ago, in 1992. We started Detroit Summer that year with young people who worked with the Gardening Angels on gardening. The Hunger Action Coalition people wanted to create an agricultural network with gardeners including elders and a wellness house some churches were doing.

We held a potluck at Kwanza in 1996, which brought together forty-two people, including Gardening Angels, Master Gardeners from Michigan State University, and city workers in Farm-a-lot and Adopt-A-Park programs and decided to create the Detroit Agricultural Network out of people who were actually doing gardening. Called on to use their imaginations and give free reign to their hopes, participants envisioned Detroit as a Garden of Eden and a gardening city rather than a gambling one; kids learning to think and developing a work ethic; children and elders working together; the weeding out of crime and hunger, cleaner, healthier neighborhoods; a cleaner environment.

The Network has been in existence for five years and includes schools, churches, elders and youth. We do a tour every August. We also made ties with the Black Farmers who had a wonderful conference here a few years ago. We wanted to connect the National Black Farmers in the South with Detroit, because many people in Detroit come from the South.

Now we're beginning to create a food security plan to include churches, health providers, universities and food providers. The idea is that we'll begin to grow our own food, do our own marketing and train young people to do marketing and other aspects of the project. It has all sorts of ramifications, and many purposes. One, to relate younger people to older people; two, to give younger people a sense of process and a contact with life which you don't have these days. Everything is all asphalt jungle. The idea is to grow community, to grow people and to grow food at the same time.

Jim Stone

The Network is a combination. The Hunger Action Coalition are the food supply providers. They've been the tip of the umbrella, where folks come together. They're a nonprofit, so we use them to launder the money. If anyone wants to donate to DAN, they write the check to the Hunger Action Coalition. The Hunger Action Coalition recently established Project Fresh through the Michigan Department of Agriculture where the home gardeners and the community gardeners and the CSAs can accept Food Stamps for a pre-measured quantity of fresh vegetables. We got some good PR out of that, the state's looking at it, and we twisted some political arms to make that happen. This pays back the people who do the work. It puts little back into their

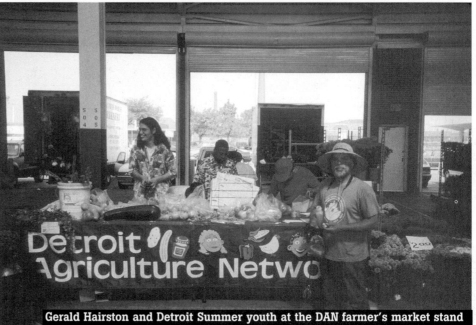

Gerald Hairston and Detroit Summer youth at the DAN farmer's market stand

pockets.

The Capuchin Soup Kitchen is real popular. Brother Rick Salmon is one of our supporters, and we've got a hoop house over there. They get volunteers to help feed the folks. Brother Rick took it one step further. He says, "The people who come to get food assistance deserve to eat well too." Instead of relying on canned goods you try to get fresh food. The Soup Kitchen acquired the vacant lot next door from the city. The City of Detroit donated it to them for a hundred bucks because there was an old skinny house on it at one time. We've got long, skinny lots, 45' by 100', and it's tough to do infill on them, especially once the neighborhood's gone down. Now the garden's an asset to the soup kitchen—there's fresh food right outside their door.

Community Supported Agriculture:
interviews with three urban farmers

Seattle, WA • Tacoma, WA • Tucson, AZ

Andrea del Moral

For most of the "winter" in Oakland, California our garden produces a steady offering of salad greens, kale, and collards. The farmers' market and grocery store are nonessential to our leafy greens diet, until the rain stops falling. In March and April, the lettuce and arugula begin to bolt uncontrollably. Kale and chard shoot up overnight, aphids attack, and all the greens taste bitter. Our yard turns into a jungle of seed pods, plants trying to reproduce as the summer heats up. Stepping off the back porch to pick the only perennial green, the purple-veined tree collards, I think of how little energy goes into getting food from the yard to the belly, even compared with "locally grown" food that comes from the farmers' market. As soon as you factor in the fossil fuel it takes to drive freshly harvested vegetables over the hills from the hotter, inland farm counties, it's nearly impossible to get energy input to balance energy output. There's so much less energy put into growing food that you can transport by walking, biking, or simply lifting your hand from plant to mouth. This is part of why I'm obsessed with urban agriculture. Energy crisis conspiracy theories aside, how food gets to people is a serious question.

Growing food in the city can be done in many ways. These three projects demonstrate that collaborative efforts among people (sharing tools, land, knowledge, labor, customers, and money) often carve out space for urban farming to thrive. This is because their structure leads people to address the common obstacles to urban food production: land tenure, food security and economic survival. The Community Supported Agriculture (CSA) and backyard farm projects in Seattle, Tacoma, and Tucson share common elements. They successfully grow large amounts of food in small areas while addressing social inequities that are aggravated by corporate industrial agriculture. They take advantage of relationships with larger institutions (like the government and nonprofits) and grassroots community groups.

In urban farming situations, a dramatic tension persists between providing income for growers and making that food accessible to low-income people. One strategy that has been gaining popularity in recent years is forming CSA farms on urban land. In a CSA model, a family buys a share of the farm's produce at the beginning of the season. This large influx of cash makes it possible for farmers to purchase seeds and soil amendments at the beginning of the season without going into debt. In return, the family (sometimes known as the "shareholder") receives a large box of seasonal vegetables, fruit, and sometimes flowers each week. While this system benefits farmers economically, some people believe it is not the best way to provide quality food at a price low-income people can afford. Sometimes farmers make a living by selling one or two crops to a fancy restaurant for a high price. While not an ideal solution, this allows them to sell their CSA shares at a lower price.

In Seattle, the Cultivating Communities project focuses on serious food production in the city and providing income for the gardeners. In Tacoma, the Guadalupe Gardens are comprehensively shaped by the culture of the neighborhood, and respond to big agriculture politics in local ways, like saving seed on all their crops. In Tucson, the Southside Food Production Network focuses on bringing food production into neighborhoods and promoting local food security. Each of these places is going about urban food production in a different way, demonstrating that there are infinite ways to bust off the chains of supermarket serfdom and free the communities we live in—every time we eat and every time we touch the urban earth.

Cultivating Communities, Seattle, Washington

We could tell when she first walked into Lottie Mott's café on Ranier Ave. South that the tall woman in jeans

43

and a shirt to get dirty in worked on the land. A self-described "urban cowgirl," 30-something Martha Goodlett met us in the Rainier Valley, a diverse, working class neighborhood in south Seattle where much of the Cultivating Communities project is centered. A farmers' market and several community gardens also thrive in the area.

Martha Goodlett says of the Cultivating Communities program, "Everybody claims it and nobody claims it." It's within the City of Seattle Department of Neighborhoods, and more specifically within the P-Patch program, which is the city's official community gardening program. There are 56 P-Patch gardens in the city including the Cultivating Communities gardens.

Martha Goodlett

The community gardening movement is strong here. The program's been around for over 25 years. The Friends of P-Patch group really goes to bat for the gardens when there are funding cuts. The criteria for P-Patch gardens is that the land needs to be guaranteed for 5 years. Some of the land is leased from individuals, some of it is on Parks Department land, and some of it has been bought by the Friends of P-Patch non-profit. Now, there isn't much more private land available, so we're looking at having gardens on public property like city and school district land. We're also starting to work with non-profit housing.

There are three types of gardens within Cultivating Communities: three CSA gardens, ten or eleven community food gardens, and two youth gardens. All of those are within Seattle Housing Authority (SHA) communities.

drawing by Greg Jalbert

Old-style public housing in S. Seattle, Cultivating communities project

Early History

In the early 1990s the Seattle Housing Authority was interested in getting gardens going on with the residents. They were concerned because the housing projects were built back in the 1940s for people working on airplanes with Boeing for WWII. It was supposed to be temporary workers' housing. They used lead paint, which was later sandblasted off, so the soil around the units has high lead levels. (Later, we put the gardens

well away from buildings and tested them again.) Residents wanted to garden and SHA had to explain they couldn't. SHA came to the Department of Neighborhoods, asking for help creating community gardens on the sites of their low-income housing. The city was really stretched and said, "we can't do this. But if the non-profit (Friends of P-Patch) could write some grants, the SHA could contribute some funds, and maybe it could happen." That was in 1995. The program started with just community gardens. Then there was a national push for job training and getting people off welfare, so the next year, 1996, we started the CSAs.

Part of the welfare reform initiative in the 1990s was to dismantle public housing. The theory was that the liberals were wrong to ghettoize everybody. The big high rise units weren't working, so they wanted to redevelop as mixed income housing. The new units are called HOPE 6; three of the four communities I'm working in are going that route and the fourth one will later. They've been controversial. The pros are that the new housing is better quality, and in principle the idea of having people around from different income levels makes sense. But my impression is that it will result in a net loss of low-income housing. Supposedly they're doing replacement housing off-site.

The old housing had a lot of open space for kids to run around. Kids from East Africa and Southeast Asia and everywhere were all out there. The parents could see their kids out in the open space and it wasn't a big deal. But in the new housing there are private yards, so where is there for the kids to go but out on the street?

The thing that's difficult is that these communities are being destroyed. Things happen so quickly and it's very stressful. It's also a headache because we build these gardens and then a few years down the road we tear them down and rebuild them. It's been interesting to be a part of this, to see things that are really hard, and to try to work within the system. SHA does appreciate it when I point out things that don't seem fair. But it's a pretty stressful process.

With the HOPE 6 projects, the amount of open space is being reduced in favor of more units. I don't want every piece of open space to be a garden because people need space to shoot hoops or just hang out. But people aren't growing food in their backyards in the new housing, because they're so small. I think there are restrictions on what the yards can look like too.

Community Gardens

To start, Cultivating Communities people walked around the community and asked people who already had gardens about joining. Bilingual people within the community helped communicate. Most of the people I work with are Southeast Asian: Cambodian, Vietnamese, and Lao. The gardeners' responsibility is to garden organically and follow the kindergarten rules.

CSA Gardens

There are three separate CSAs; each one is about 1/2 acre. We have 24 shares at each garden. We charge $350 for 18 weeks. Most people split that with another family. They get two bags of groceries a week. There tend to be more greens than people want and less root vegetables. The first year, it was mostly radishes and mustard greens, and people said "Boy I really learned how to cook with radishes!" We have biweekly meetings, with two or three staff there who are interpreters and help solve problems. At the first meetings we talked about how we were going to divide the money. Would each gardener have different customers, or work in teams? Now we use those meetings to figure out what to plant and give the gardeners information from the customer surveys, like "Stop giving us so many Chinese mustard greens." About root crops, the gardeners say, "Oh, too slow, too slow."

The model here is gardening, not farming. Not that they won't help each other out, but everyone has their own individual plot. Each site has its own customers. Keeping these gardens going is a lot more staff-intensive than the community gardens. The first year takes a lot of time, 20 or 30 hours a week, the second year maybe 10 hours, the third year, maybe five. We're trying to get recipes developed so customers know what to do with everything. But the problem is that most of the gardeners use the vegetables with meat, and the customers are looking for how to make vegetable dishes with them.

I try to work with the gardeners based on what they know how to grow and start building on that. I tell them what the customers said, and for a while I felt like I was just banging my head against the wall, that

nothing was really changing, but I think it slowly is changing now. We get really good attendance at the gardeners' meetings. We have at least one gathering per year between the customers and the gardeners.

Economic Justice in the Garden

The $350 price for a share is not super high for a CSA but it's not low either. Other CSAs in the Seattle area charge up to $600 for twenty weeks. We let SHA residents know that if they want to join, we'll give them a discount. We don't actively recruit them because we want the gardeners to earn as much as possible.

The gardeners get 75% of the income from shares, but people don't support themselves doing this. Most of the gardeners are over 55, so this is more about life than about a job. I deal with the customers, the marketing, and the money.

In terms of making organic, local food accessible for lower income people, I think farmers' markets are a better bet. I

drawing by Greg Jalbert

HOPE 6 housing and one of the Cultivating Communities Gardens

don't believe that the CSA is the only way. The Columbia City farmers' market right here takes WIC coupons and food stamps. One third of the sales that come through there are for low income people. The point of the CSA is to help people connect, and to get financial stability for farmers.

High Point Garden

Fourteen gardeners make up the High Point CSA. They pool all their produce for the shares. We work with Delridge Neighborhoods Development Association. That's a middle to lower middle income area in West Seattle. Through them we've reached out to more granola-type families that like coming to the garden. They have kids, they'll share their share with another family, or a church will buy a share for a family. This garden seems to be rising to the community-building potential of CSAs, because this group of customers cares about coming to the garden, connecting to the process of growing food and getting to know the gardeners.

Rainier Vista Garden

There are just two gardeners here, even though the area of the garden is the same as High Point. Most of our customers in this garden are from the Mt. Baker community, where the average price of a house is $700,000 to $800,000. They're co-op shoppers; they like the idea of supporting a garden. They want healthy food, but food security isn't such an obvious issue. The CSA members can afford access to healthy food at the co-op. The real success of this garden is the economic opportunity it has provided for its gardeners. One of them made maybe $6000 last year with a farmers' market booth, the CSA, and cut flowers. But she's under a lot of pressure as the only breadwinner in her family. She has two other jobs now so she probably won't do so much this year.

Holly Park Garden

There are 20 gardeners at this garden. They divide up by language group—Cambodians pool their vegetables for some shares, Vietnamese for others, like that. The same people gardening for the CSA have a plot for their families too—they plant their traditional crops. At Holly Park we work through Earth Ministry, an environmental interfaith organization. We reach out through congregations. We work with St. Therese Catholic Church, which by no means consists of affluent people as far as I can tell. We also do a drop at St. Andrews Episcopal Church in north Seattle.

The reason we got the land at Holly Park was for job training. As part of the Holly Park redevelopment there was some money for resident services. They created a "campus of learners." They're trying to get job-training people working with social service people. Out of that came the youth gardens. It's starting off slowly. We've got maybe fifty kids at different times participating.

Youth Gardens

We're using VISTA volunteers to get it going. We have two strategies. First, we work with youth service providers. They're looking for programs. Second, we're trying to establish youth and family gardens. These gardens are a way for parents and kids to connect, especially parents who come from agricultural backgrounds. The kids are mainly eight to twelve years old. I don't work directly on that program so I can't speak of it so well.

Lessons from the Urban Cowgirl

The philosophy I use is doing the work with the community, really having them making the decisions about how we're going to do things. "How are we going to divide up the land? Where's the water system going to be?" We're giving them information to help them make decisions and trying to find who to collaborate with. It has been critical to keep building relationships with the SHA and all the different groups so that it fits together with their plans. SHA has been very supportive of the gardens. They realize they play a role in community building. With the new housing, there's no net loss of garden space (even though it's socially very different in relation to the houses). If we hadn't kept a good rela-

tionship with them, the gardens might not be part of the new housing.

Guadalupe Gardens, Tacoma, Washington

There's a mysterious connection between amazon women and urban agriculture projects in the Pacific Northwest. Carrie Little coordinated the necklace of CSA gardens that dot the sloping side of Tacoma's Hilltop neighborhood for many years. Her determination continues to inspire those around her to see potential in the broken down land of the inner city. Like Martha Goodlett, Carrie has managed to juggle urban food production projects with independent rural farm endeavors. Both women mention in passing the six or ten acres of farmland they're cultivating outside of town "in their spare time." The passion that drives them to such ambitions burns fiery through their urban projects. Guadalupe Gardens is a thriving example.

Carrie Little

When I came here in 1993, there were little plots where people would adopt a spot, community garden style. A lot of folks would plant things and then never come back and weed them. So this other gal and I picked up the pieces, got a little organized, and said, "Hey, let's see what we can do at the farmers' market," and made a thousand bucks without even trying.

CSA Farmer Chuks in La Grande Garden, Tacoma, WA

Economic Justice—the CSA

In 1995, we started gardening as a CSA farm. Each share costs $275 for a 20-week season, and $40 extra for flowers. There are 55 shares, grown on 1/2 acre. Most of our customers are people from nearby. We give away about five shares a year to very local low income people. The point is not to make a ton of money. It's tricky though, because with the people we want to serve, there's no profit in selling shares. It's good to get sponsorships or donations from more wealthy shareholders. If you work it so you're under the umbrella of a nonprofit, then those donations can be written off. It's a much more sustainable way to go than grants. Grants are good for buying tools, getting a piece of land, but for the long term it's better to do sponsorships, or one big event a year like a big feast, where you sell raffle tickets or whatever. Having some kind of product like basil for a restaurant can make up the difference.

Our expenses are pretty low. We pay for three gardeners and water from the city. Then there is a lot of volunteer labor. We have work parties; every other week District Court community service folks come out. They come out here in their truck, with their port-a-potty and the volunteers, and they have to spend eight hours. At first they're dragging, "Oh god we gotta garden." So I pair them off and give them a task, and I go back and check on them in 15 minutes, and whoever their partner is, they're starting to have conversations, and you say, "Oh yeah? So you gardened with you grandmother. Hmm. So what did you learn?" They start talking about it—it's incredible. And a lot of them come back and volunteer later.

The gardens produce tons of food. Different crops are more productive than others from year to year. Last year it was garlic. This year it was tomatoes. Beats me why. We usually get blight. But last year I must have donated 5,000 pounds, and that was after giving away 10-pound bags for eight straight weeks until people said "Enough already!"

We've gotten to the point where we don't have to buy seed. We save seed on most of our varieties. We're involved in a lot of seed-saving projects: The Farmer Cooperative Germplasm Project in Oregon, the Seed Savers' Exchange, the seed growers for Abundant Life Seed Foundation. We save some seed on carrots. No brassicas although I have a killer supply of purple broccoli. The mizuna just goes wild here. A lot of people think that seed growing is inaccessible, but it's not. It makes so much sense. I can grow something here and

have its closest relative in that garden three blocks away. Corn, for example. I did a midnight blue sweet corn that was awesome, and I had a red flint corn down there. I didn't want to play the game of covering them up, or chopping the tassels, and it worked.

These gardens are important to this community, they're important to individuals. If there's a time when I can't work the land, I will be a CSA shareholder. It's just that valuable.

> **A lot of folks would plant things and then never come back and weed them. So this other gal and I picked up the pieces, got a little organized, and said, "Hey, let's see what we can do at the farmers' market," and made a thousand bucks without even trying.**
>
> **—Carrie Little, Guadalupe Gardens CSA**

Southside Food Production Network, Tucson, Arizona

"If you look at a map that has a bunch of cities on it," says Varga Garland, "there are lines drawn between all the cities. That's what we're doing with food security and localizing the global food system." In 1997, the Southside Food Production Network (SFPN) formed out of conversations about creating local food systems. In 1998, they received funding from the USDA Community Food Security Project Grant. That grant funds three part-time salaries. A fourth salary comes from the Southside Food Bank, where the SFPN office and one of the community gardens are.

Varga Garland

The goals of a local food system involve a lot of levels of knowledge and information. A huge amount of what we do involves local food production and sales. We also work with communities and schools to change people's ideas about food in this area. We've worked with neighborhoods on getting grocery stores back in, and creating an awareness of local food insecurity and what we can do about it.

Community Gardens

The "workhorse" of our program is the Food Bank garden, which is in its fourth year. The produce from this garden is sold at a garden market table at the Food Bank on Tuesday mornings. Other gardeners in the neighborhood bring produce to sell too. They keep the money they make, and the money from the Food Bank garden produce goes back into the gardens. The garden market table is an opportunity for us to talk with people who might want backyard gardens, and to talk about growing food in our area. We buy seedlings for backyard gardens from that market.

The Pueblo garden is supported by Americorps members who work at that school. They've been there for three years. The garden includes a ramada, picnic tables under it, and water from the building to the garden. It's about 150 yards from the building to the garden—that's a long way! There are two gardens at the school, and both are being used for curriculum. Former students—teenagers now—are mentors for the kids who're still there. They planted about sixty trees a while back, along a 1/2-mile-long path into the garden. They're working to make it a park available to all the Southside community.

Quincy Douglas Community Center is about a year and a half old. During the planning stage, people in the South Park neighborhood asked to have a garden as part of the center. Because of SFPN's earlier work in the neighborhood, the city paid for the excavation, fencing, shade structures, and irrigation for the garden. We've been working with the community to develop the garden, in conjunction with the rest of their programs. There's a lot of opportunity to work with community members who come to Quincy Douglas already. They have a seniors breakfast and lunch program five days a week, and there's an after school and teen program out of a public housing facility nearby.

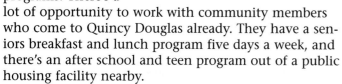
Food Bank Garden, Tucson, AZ
photo by Blake Nemec

Backyard Gardens

In Backyard Gardens, we bring materials and technical expertise about gardening in the desert. We make sure that we don't create environments where the water bill goes up so high that there's not a benefit to growing vegetables in your backyard. We help people build lots of compost too, because we have crummy soil here. If we amend it, by creating compost at our homes and getting it donated, then we can manage.

Growing Food Where the Kids Are

We do the same thing around backyard gardens with an elementary school, Los Niños, and a middle school, Utterback. This year Los Niños is putting in about half a dozen backyard gardens in the neighborhood. We play the same role—we provide the needed material elements and the desert gardening knowledge.

At Utterback Middle School, a science teacher and a service learning teacher wanted to make it possible for kids to do community service and applied learning in science and math during school time. Those classes go into people's backyards, and we bring all the materials and expertise. The kids bring their good strong hands

and enthusiasm, and work with the women with yards in Sunland Vista neighborhood.

Mujeres Unidas

Mujeres Unidas is a group of 15 to 20 women doing a variety of good things for themselves. They all live on the South Nogales Highway, which is a very rural area just south of Tucson. They came together a number of years ago around the bookmobile that the library sent around. They got a grant to build a ramada from the Pro Neighborhoods organization. One of the people who had been working with Mujeres Unidas worked with us, and she suggested we could work with them on a community garden. This was a group of women who had organized themselves, were looking for resources in the community, and we just happened to be one of the resources they were looking for.

We put a community garden in with them at the ramada, and they discovered that they would prefer to have backyard gardens. In order to be able to do that, they organized backyard garden parties. The women go as a group to somebody's backyard on a Saturday morning. We bring the compost and tools and manure, often the seeds, straw, shadecloth, hoses—everything they need for the garden.

The kind of work that began with Mujeres Unidas has expanded to include work at the elementary school where many of these women go for ESL literacy class. Americorps members who are part of the literacy program work on the garden at the school, as well.

Mujeres Unidas do a lot of other things together too. We've worked with them in developing a sewing class. They got a grant and bought four sewing machines. They all do lots of handwork, but working with sewing machines and patterns was new, and we've been able to help them with that too.

Collaborations

As with almost every project, there are limited resources for SFPN work. So we have to be strategic in what kind of collaboration we do. First, we figure out how much of a plan somebody has. Sometimes what they really want is support. They have resources, but they need information about gardening in the desert more than they need physical help. We determine what we can do based on how many resources somebody is bringing. Human resources are the best, because we can access most of the other resources. Sometimes they have limited human resources but they're doing real problem solving about getting other kinds of resources. It depends on how problem solving oriented the folks we're working with are.

An example of the collaborations we do is that we've just started talking with the

the Food Bank garden

the Desert Vista community college campus about a garden-based chef education program. They also want to include some very low income neighborhoods nearby. We're trying to figure out how to coordinate the resources they've got. We've known all along that if we could sell some of our organic produce to the fancy restaurants in town we could subsidize our income. The chef who runs that program has contacts with all those restaurants. We hope we'll be able to help them connect with the nearby neighborhoods, and also connect with chefs, so it'll work out for everyone.

We also work with the city. We've been challenged by the idiosyncrasies of a bureaucracy of the city; at the same time, having all their resources is wonderful. They have recently passed a new regulation to pick up green waste every other week, and to start a city composting program. Then they're going to provide everyone in the city who grows food with compost, and they'll deliver it. You have to have compost in this desert city, and we can't make enough of it out of our own gardens.

"Hunger's easy"

In theory, if people are hungry and you feed them, problem solved. But food security isn't easy. Community food security is defined by the National Community Food Security Coalition as "All persons obtaining, at all times, a culturally acceptable and nutritionally adequate diet through local, non-emergency sources." We're fortunate to have a food bank here that is very willing to talk about a local food system, and to get people to stop paying attention only to hunger. All the work that's done here at the food bank is going to make a difference here in Tucson. The Food Bank recently received a grant to do food stamp outreach, and we're going to do Food Bank production education as well. Arizona has just passed authorization to participate in federal programs. In a few years we will be able to take food stamps at the market garden table.

Our goal is to have a local food system that people are aware of and participate in. We want a local food network that pays attention to farmers on the outskirts, just south and north of us. Community education is important: getting people to pay attention to where their food comes from, what they can do to influence where their food comes from, and getting people to grow their own food. If you can just manage to get through May and June [hot summer months before the monsoon rains come] all the rest of the months are a piece of cake! Once you figure out how to amend the soil, you can grow things. Then you figure out how to harvest water, so you're not reducing groundwater to produce food. You don't want the exchange of vegetables for water to be a loss. This may be a lot of figuring out, but you can do it!

mural at the Food Bank garden

Some people are ready for all this. There's a bunch of people who aren't. That's all right. We've been on a pretty steep learning curve ourselves for the last three years, so we'll just put other people on that learning curve and then we'll all be on it.

Struggles

mural showing environmental justice issues in San Francisco's Bayview Hunters Point neighborhood

Roxbury, MA • Bronx, NY • Tacoma, WA

"We should have known better. Friends told us about urban gardens connected to the Martin De Porres Catholic Worker in San Francisco. They were all bulldozed to make way for development years ago. Imagine the difference if they had held onto them. Now the forces of gentrification even want the soup kitchen to move out of "their" neighborhood.

—Bruce Triggs, co-founder of the Guadalupe Land Trust

"We've watched and been inspired by the cliffhanger saga of the Homeless Garden Project in Santa Cruz. They were operating on borrowed City land, until the City changed its mind and the whole operation had to move! This could easily have killed the operation and scattered the community they'd gathered; but they managed to find new sites, and as of now, they continue to inspire.

"While staying at the New York Catholic Worker, I visited the neighborhood gardens on the Lower East Side. I remember walking around and finding different ones, a kaleidoscope of form, from simple lots with a few crumbling brick borders to one unforgettable wrought iron fence with walkways hanging above the street. Glass and colored plastic artifacts were strung up in trees and woven in between plants. Murals and flags showed community support for Puerto Rican independence. I came away raving about a crazy tower made of two by fours and dumpstered materials, mocking the skyscrapers of the city. It defiantly stood three stories tall in the middle of a garden lot, flying a flag off scrap wood at the top. Most of the New York gardens had signs stating the city's intent to demolish, and announcing desperate meetings to protect them.

"We've heard rumors and reports of bulldozers crushing the work of generations, and of communities coming together to say 'No.' They inspire with the significance of what we have to do, the power of community tied to place, and life wrung from cracks in city pavement." —Bruce Triggs

In the last five years, gentrification has changed the face of entire neighborhoods in cities like New York and San Francisco. Low income neighborhoods such as West Philadelphia and the Hilltop neighborhood in Tacoma have also felt the pressure of development.

Following the massive burnouts of certain inner-city neighborhoods in the 1970s, neighbors organized to turn rubble-filled lots into gardens and community gathering places. City governments often see this neighborhood improvement as the primary role of urban gardens. But as members of the Bronx United Gardeners point out, the city's bottom line is money. The city views urban gardens as a way to bring up property values while saving the city the cost of maintaining the lots. Once gardens, arts organizations and other grassroots efforts have made a neighborhood desirable to yuppies and their accompanying clubs, restaurants and oxygen bars, the city has no qualms about evicting low-income residents and bulldozing gardens.

Gardeners also recognize the neighborhood improvement that gardens bring. Gardens provide spaces for people to organize around tenants rights and environmental justice issues. In Roxbury, Massachusetts, youth from The Food Project mapped all the gardens in the Dudley neighborhood and educated gardeners about the dangers of lead and other contaminants in the soil. The youth worked with several gardeners to remediate their soils and went on to lobby the city government for free compost, multilingual signage about the dangers of lead, and zoning for green space in new developments.

This local organizing pays off when the eviction notices come from the city. The Bronx United Gardeners have banded together to successfully stop the destruction of their ten gardens for more than two years. In addition to preserving the gardens, this struggle has made activists out of many gardeners. Through the struggle for gardens, gardeners have gained valuable tools that they are using to continue the greening of their cities. As Detroit activist Grace Boggs explains, "I see this whole business of beginning to use vacant lots for growing food and for growing community as a way that we're going rebuild Detroit in a totally different way from how Downtown thinks they're going to rebuild it. Downtown thinks in terms of luxury gambling casinos. We see it from the ground up."

the Bronx United Gardeners

We're Here To Stay

the Bronx United Gardeners

We, the Bronx United Gardeners are a coalition of gardeners from ten urban community gardens in the Morrisania neighborhood of the South Bronx. We formed a group in the spring of 1999 in response to the news that the city government wanted to bulldoze our gardens, some of which are over thirty years old, and all of which are incredibly important parts of our community. City Housing Preservation and Development (HPD) wrote us letters saying that we should take everything out of our gardens and stop planting. Instead of leaving quietly as they hoped we would, we have stood up to city government and through a variety of tactics, preserved our gardens for two years and counting. This article is the story of our neighborhood, of our gardens, and of our fight to preserve our green spaces and help gardeners from around the city do the same.

Bronx Burnout: Before the Gardens

Just as it is now, the South Bronx was the poorest congressional district in the country during the 60s and 70s. Cordelia Gilford of the C.S. 134 Community Improvement Garden remembers Morrisania as it was when she moved into her current residence in 1960. "I used to live in a Manhattan apartment, but then the city took our building and demolished it to build housing projects. So I moved to 171st St. to another apartment, but the city took that for the same reason. So then in 1960, my husband and I scraped together the money for a house so we wouldn't have to move anymore. I've lived there ever since. Everyone knew each other back then. It was a lot of young families."

In the early 1970s, the whole country fell into a bad economic period of "stagfla-

tion." The New York city government went bankrupt and cut back on services in poor neighborhoods and communities of color. Verna Judge of the Debaron Civic Association garden explains, "The area was 'redlined.' This basically meant that the city was going to let it go down the tubes and cut off services. Landlords would just stop making repairs but continue collecting rent. We called it 'milking the building.' You didn't see them stopping anyone's garbage pick up on the Upper East Side. They blamed the poor, said we were living in filth, but really it was city policy." The official name of the policy was "planned shrinkage." The idea was to pull out public funds and services from these areas so that poor people would be forced to leave, and eventually, when the economy got better, redevelop the area as a middle-class suburb of Manhattan.

Gardeners describe the Bronx of the early 1970s as

a BUG meeting in a Bronx garden

photo by Jeff Conant

"bombed out" and a "trash dump" and explain that landlords would pay off people to burn down the buildings so they could collect insurance. "Rubble filled lots were left behind," Jim Austen of C.S. 134 Garden explains, "People would start dumping old cars, frigidaires, trash bags right next to where people were living." On Verna Judge's block, "there were only three occupied buildings, two were private houses and one was apartments. All the rest was either abandoned buildings, vacant lots, or piles of rubble." Austen agrees. "It was a vicious cycle," he says, "and it was all about money for the city government, money for the landlords."

Bronx Community Gardens: Truly Grassroots

Despite the city's plan to chase out poor people by denying them services, residents like Cordelia Gilford, Verna Judge, and Tex Smith stayed. Cordelia explains, "I struggled hard for my house, and I wasn't going to leave that easy. I love this area. If I left, I'd be abandoning the area the same way as the landlords and the city government. This is where our community was." Verna Judge has similar feelings. "I had a vested interest in this neighborhood. I wanted to be here working with my people through the Debaron Civic Association. I might have been able to afford to leave, but not everyone else could."

Both the C.S. 134 garden and the Debaron Civic Association garden began in 1967 without sponsorship from the city.

"We just got out there and did what we had to do. It was city land, but they didn't seem to care what happened to it, and we did. So we took it over," explains Cordelia Gilford.

Residents of the blocks around the garden started helping out, and soon both sites were thriving green spaces. All over the city, from East New York in Brooklyn, to the Lower East Side and Harlem in Manhattan, to the South Bronx, residents began cleaning up rubble filled lots, and planting them with food. Many garden founders had recently moved from farms in Puerto Rico or the southeastern US, and they brought their agricultural skills with them. Ms. Mattie from the Geneva McFadden community garden explains, "It was just natural. I was used to tasty, home grown vegetables, not that cardboard they sell down at the store. And I already knew how to work hard, how to plant, how to save seeds. It just made sense to start gardening once I moved up here from down South."

In 1978, the city government responded to this grassroots movement by forming Operation Greenthumb. Over the years, Operation Greenthumb has provided valuable materials and services to keep gardens alive. At the same time, some say that at its inception, the city department was a way of co-opting a movement. Gardeners had formerly squatted city government land, potentially giving them adverse possession rights according to some lawyers. Once the government got involved, gardeners signed leases in which they agreed to leave if ordered to. The advent of a city program catering to gardens also divided the garden movement into "legal" gardens holding leases on city owned land and "illegal" gardens on either private land, or on city land but without a lease. These theories should in no way detract from the fact that Operation Greenthumb presently provides an incalculable amount of support to community gardeners, making it economically feasible for those without funds to start a garden.

From 1967 on, neighborhood residents banded together and formed the ten gardens which now make up the Bronx United Gardens. Whether formed in the late

In the Bronx, many buildings like this one stand vacant the city manufactures a "housing crunch" to justify building new housing on top of gardens.

photo: More Gardens!

"The area was 'redlined.' This basically meant that the city was going to let it go down the tubes and cut off services. Landlords would just stop making repairs but continue collecting rent. We called it 'milking the building.' They blamed the poor, said we were living in filth, but really it was city policy."

60s as ghetto burnout was occurring, or a decade and a half later on the vacant lots left behind as a result, the gardens' stories are similar. The gardens rose out of a community need and were built through the labor and love of residents. While gardeners around the city responded to the lack of green space and the rise of abandoned lots, other community groups formed to squat or homestead the many abandoned buildings in the area. The city had underestimated the grassroots determination of people to stay in their neighborhoods and make them both livable and affordable.

City Government: Putting Profit Before Gardens

Gardens provide many benefits to the community, so why does the city want to get rid of them? "Very simply, money," says James Austen. "The city government wants to expand their tax base by building middle income houses so there's more money in the district. Officials are getting pressured by the city construction lobbyists, who also make donations to campaigns. It's all a vicious cycle. It's greed and it's been around for ages, and I doubt its going any where anytime soon." Most gardeners seem to agree that the bottom line of the city government's official story is profit.

green space. Second, it unfortunately established a pattern of privatization as the effective way to make gardens permanent. There was still no process by which gardens could be preserved, other than to be bought at high prices, with the city choosing the buyer. As of now, the city is refusing negotiations with the original non-profits that bought the gardens.

Marie Brooks of the Jackson-Forrest Garden describes the city's strategy: "After the auction, the city realized they had to be more sneaky. They want to bulldoze just as many gardens now as they ever did, only they're

> **"The city government wants to expand their tax base by building middle income houses so there's more money in the district. Officials are getting pressured by the city construction lobbyists, who also make donations to campaigns. It's all a vicious cycle. It's greed and it's been around for ages, and I doubt its going any where anytime soon."**
>
> **—James Austen**

doing it development by development, one by one." In February 2000, the city bulldozed the Esperanza community garden in the Lower East Side to make way for luxury housing, through a small development plan. All over the city, the New York City Department of Housing Preservation and Development (HPD) has been quietly picking developers for small scale projects built on top of community gardens.

The city government has been after the gardens for years, but since 1999, they seem to have stepped up a policy of garden destruction. In the spring of 1999, the city tried to auction off 112 community gardens around the city to the highest bidder. Gardeners and their supporters rose up in opposition to this brutal policy. Through a combination of rallies, direct action and civil disobedience they got the public's attention. The day before the scheduled auction, two non-profit groups were able to reach a deal with the city to buy the 112 gardens, preserving them as part of private land trusts. This outcome had two effects. First, it showed the city government that garden destruction would not be easy, and that people would rise up, speak out, organize and agitate in defense of

Photo: More Gardens!

A BUG rally in front of City Hall

In 1999, HPD announced that it would accept proposals from private developers for projects built on top of lots in the area, including all ten of the community gardens in an eight block radius. HPD stipulated that the developments would have to be 2-3 family row houses, for a middle income home buyer range. Though they say gardens are being brushed aside to make way for much needed affordable housing, in reality this housing is being sold to people with over three times the neighborhood average income. In addition, it is a low-density model, which does not provide a large amount of new housing to the neighborhood. It is also being built on community gardens, rather than on the many vacant lots in the community district, or by rehabilitating the existing abandoned buildings. "I went around and took pictures of all the vacant lots right around my garden," Tex says. "There's one across the street, one down the block, one on the other side of the block and one down the adjacent street— they're everywhere! But for some reason the city wants to bulldoze us!" Some say that gardens are being targeted because its less expensive to build on vacant land than to rehabilitate abandoned buildings. Others say its because the city just doesn't care what people in the neighborhood think. Some say it's politically motivated, because gardens function as organizing sites for neighborhood residents to fight the city on a variety of issues.

"We are not afraid to speak the truth to the city government and anyone else who will listen. And no one can shut me up when I start speaking the truth."
—Cordelia Gilford

BUG: Organizing and Agitating

Despite the city's plan to destroy the ten gardens that are part of the Bronx United Gardeners, gardeners have held on for over two years. When gardeners first received letters from HPD asking them to vacate and telling them that their gardens would be destroyed, gardeners held a meeting at Verna Judge's garden to discuss the situation. They decided not to stop planting or holding events in their gardens. And they decided to stand up to the city and defend their gardens. Out of this initial meeting the Bronx United Gardeners (BUG) was formed.

BUG has used several tactics in garden defense. This has involved a combination of organizing within the community, and applying pressure to city officials who wish to destroy the gardens. There were community tours, community parties, meetings, and flyers. BUG has also put pressure on the city through media coverage, visiting offices unannounced with lists of demands, rallying with 200 people on the steps of city hall, letter writing, and speaking out at public hearings. BUG also worked in coalition with other garden groups from around the city to organize a huge rally at city hall in May, 2001.

One of the most interesting things that has happened in BUG is an exchange of learning between older community gardeners and young activists. "I started out as an activist, fighting broad ideological issues, and I wasn't very connected to my local community," explains Isabel Moore. Through BUG, I have learned how to grow things, and I've learned more about the Bronx." Cordelia Gilford, on the other hand, started out as a resource for community gardeners and neighbors who had not attended many rallies in the past.

"Now I've spoken in front of a rally of over 200 people on behalf of BUG. I know how to speak to the media as well." Younger members of BUG agree that they have much to learn from the older gardeners' experience and sense of history. Older gardeners say that they have gotten energy to keep fighting from the young people who have gotten involved.

"We have been successful so far because the 'squeaky wheel gets the oil' as they say," declares James. "And we have stood together. In unity there is strength," adds Verna. Cordelia notes, "We haven't backed down. We are persistent and we know our facts. We've learned every bit of the city government process affecting our gardens," she says.

"We are not afraid to speak the truth to the city government and anyone else who will listen," Ms. Mattie says. "And no one can shut me up when I start speaking the truth."

Our Current Status

"Despite the fact that we've held off the bulldozers for over two years, the city is still trying to take our gardens." says Tex. At the time of the writing [May, 2001] at the city council level, HPD and their private developers have gotten approval from the Land Use Committee, but not the Finance committee. The Finance committee has not denied the proposal, and HPD continues to lobby for its passage. At the state level, State Attorney general Elliott Spitzer has sued city government on behalf of all unprotected gardens city wide, and though the city is still fighting to have the case dismissed, BUG gardens are currently protected by a Temporary Restraining Order.

"It is amazing that BUG has gotten this far in the struggle," a downtown garden activist remarks. "It is rare for city council to be under so much pressure that they hold off on a full decision for over two years."

"Our gardens have been here over thirty years," says Verna. "We don't plan on giving up this fight easily. We plan on saving our gardens for our great grandchildren to enjoy, even if it takes a struggle."

Growing Guadalupe Gardens, Trusting in the Land

Tacoma, WA

Bruce Triggs

First of all, I should reveal that I'm not a gardener. I want to be, wish I was, but I go out and last maybe two hours before I get frustrated and distracted. Maybe I'm just lazy. Maybe I'll grow into it like my grandparents and mom— go out in the garden whenever I can— but I want to make sure people credit the real gardeners. I've mostly been thankful looking out my window on the view, taking life and food, and putting in a few hours here and there. (Some years I've done better, and I did help paint the beautiful mural on the back of Guadalupe House. It brightens the winter garden, and reminds us of summers to come.) I've had the privilege of living here eight-plus years, and spent these last two helping clarify and strengthen the gardens' land situation.

Guadalupe House and Gardens

Guadalupe House, located on the edge of Tacoma's Hilltop neighborhood, has for years been an outpost of hope in a community of struggles. Named after Our Lady of Guadalupe in the 1970s when Ann Flagg opened her house to poor women, for ten years it was known as the "G Street Community," where people with mental illness lived together with community members. Those folks joined the house to its neighbor and, after adding the entropy of a fire and subsequent rebuilding, left us with the current 14 bedroom architectural improvisation we live in today.

In 1989 the property was taken over by the Tacoma Catholic Worker, an intentional community committed to voluntary simplicity (no salaries), non-violent social activism, and living together with the poor. We invite formerly homeless guests to stay with us based on their needs and "fit" in the community. Some stay for a few days, others have been here years; some are easy to live

with, some hard. We see all sorts of problems, from people who got hurt at work and can't pay rent to folks who've been sleeping under bridges for decades. We have several houses in the block near Guadalupe House.

Our gardens began with the help of a man named Gene Wick. He had lived in the greenhouse of a former garden he helped run on the block, and he eventually died in our house from cancer. His window here looked out on what's still the only garden owned by us outright, and that first plot is named after him. Over the years the project expanded and changed with different people and energy. It went through a "community garden" phase, where neighbors adopted plots and planted what they wanted. Then, in 1991, Karreen Perrin, Carrie Little and Bill Bichsel started to build the garden's land base by negotiating use agreements with owners of neighboring "abandoned" lots. This benefited owners, by keeping the city from hassling them to keep them clean, and we got to start gardens cheap.

mural and photos by Bruce Triggs, montage by cleo

Once garden volunteers cleared years of debris and blackberries, these new gardens grew into a Community Supported Agriculture (CSA) program that provided groceries for up to fifty families and some income to the folks doing the work. Several gardeners came from our house, and had both housing and spending money while they were here. Meanwhile, the gardens were a way for the community to adopt and change blighted properties by making them into something productive and beautiful. From magnets for trash and junk (lots of drug-use in those lots) the gardens became a place of life in the rough and sometimes dangerous city. The House and Gardens have been complementary— though not frictionless— partners in improving life in our neighborhood.

Borrowed Land

In the last few years, we faced— or rather finally began facing—the problems of gardening in our changing neighborhood. We'd never known how to respond to the encroaching development in Downtown Tacoma. Our busy lives didn't stop development's creep up the hill towards our precariously "borrowed" land. We knew it was coming when the new university campus moved in.

We started to participate nervously during a re-write of the downtown zoning laws. We went to meetings, and pushed somewhat successfully for gardens and urban open space to be included in their plans. We even kept much of our neighborhood from being zoned to allow 300-ft office buildings.

Then, last year, a trusted owner of two of our gardens suddenly sold to a condominium developer! The gardens had never been safe, but when it finally happened, we were devastated. Carrie worked with volunteers to transplant hundreds of flowers from that garden. And we suddenly got more serious about protecting the remaining space.

At the end of last season I stood in the moonlight overlooking the St. Stephen's garden from the street above. I watched the sunflower stalks and the rows covered for winter, and I promised to do what I could to protect that place. Talking with Carrie, she said they were almost done "putting the gardens to sleep for the winter," and I thought, "If we don't save them, they may not ever wake up."

Own It!

If I can say only one thing about urban gardening now, my long term perspective is: "Own Your Land!" As we meet (and meet and meet) to set up our Land Trust, the biggest frustration is not legal paper work or group process. The pain comes from missing opportunities, seeing how we "could have" saved land and gardens if we had only started sooner. Thoughts of, "We had the money to buy that garden last fall, but people on that committee didn't know we had the funds!" That is a terrible story.

Our busy lives didn't stop development's creep up the hill towards our precariously "borrowed" land. We knew it was coming when the new university campus moved in.

Bruce designed this mural—it's a representation of our neighborhood here. It's a weird street, because it's a dead end at this point, but people can come from that direction, flying downhill at a million miles an hour sometimes. The mural's got a heartbeat that starts it, and then there's a dead end and a stop sign "fear", and people's hands are being held by these chains, but they're sharing bread, which is kind of symbolic of this whole area.

But the chains are being broken by gardens, and then by people working together. A lot of these characters here are people from this community—the priest Bix who spent a year in jail for putting a red handprint on the School of the America's sign, the woman in the pink outline who passed on lived in the house down below. You'll never guess who I am—painted by the compost. Kareen is my friend who worked on the project a lot in the beginning, and she's still around—she's the flower girl. There's all kinds of different characters. -Carrie Little

57

Most people are like us and don't act until there's a crisis. Please don't follow our example here! Start as soon as you plant, and work to control the land. Gardens can sustain and empower communities, feeding them and holding them together. They are worth too much to risk them if it's avoidable. You are investing love and life in the earth. We've learned how quickly that work can be erased. Take steps early so your gardens won't go to waste under pavement.

Gardens span decades; healthy farms can be passed down through generations for centuries! We need to look at them with the long-term vision of building soil and community over years. The only way to do that is to control the land and protect it.

There are too many stories of life-giving urban places that could have been saved, but weren't. Communities wait to try to save their land until it's under pressure by development (read: worth something) and by then it's much harder. We lost our two gardens because we didn't know things would move as fast as they did.

We build gardens out of work and love in communities where land isn't valued, but ownership of that garden land is vital to protect it from the unstable future.

Gardens span decades; healthy farms can be passed down through generations for centuries! Urban gardens can and should have the same longevity. We need to look at them with the long-term vision of building soil and community over years. The only way to do that is to control the land and protect it.

We've been meeting monthly for a year or so to organize a land trust here. It's amazing how long it takes just to decide on a name! We're on the way to file for state non-profit corporation status, then to get 501(c)3 tax-exemption with the feds. This is a mystery to me, and I struggle with it technically, morally and politically. But because we want to own the land, and want to access money to buy it, this is what we've chosen to do.

We are creating a board of directors and writing articles of incorporation and bylaws to become an officially

recognized not-for-profit corporation. We've borrowed from other land trusts to write those documents. And we're getting a friendly lawyer to look over our work and give us advice. We figure we'll have it filed and operating in six months to a year. Friends in the land-trust movement helped us to get this far. Equity Trust in Connecticut is closest to what we're doing since they specialize in urban agriculture and protecting CSA-type farms. Institute for Community Economics (ICE) in Vermont is very knowledgeable and works with low-income housing land trusts. We met our lawyer friend through one of the local conservation land trusts.

We found that there is a gap in Land Trust-dom between "community" land trusts that mostly do housing, and "conservation" land trusts like the Nature Conservancy that preserve open space, wetlands and forests. Urban gardens fall neatly into the crevasse between those two. We're working with folks like Equity to support linking people back to nature, but right here in the city where they live.

Chuks, Tacoma urban farmer, in the greenhouse at La Grande Garden

The biggest event recently has been our growing cooperation with a religious-based low-income housing developer called Mercy Housing. Together, we're on the verge of signing a deal where we'll go to the city and other funders, and (with money they give us) Mercy will build 25 units of housing in our neighborhood (that could otherwise fill up with high-priced condos). Next to the houses, we'll preserve our largest garden. Partnership is cool!

This process took time, with miscommunication and mistrust along the way, but the result looks really good. We successfully took this project to the local Neighborhood Council (which decides how to spend some city funds) and were granted $150,000 to pay for the garden part of this project! Now we go to the City Council and other low-income housing funders to secure the funds for the housing. This is exciting!

Mercy Housing designers even want to build a rain-catch and gray-water recovery system in from the beginning. This will hopefully cut water costs to the gardens dramatically, and we can't wait to see this integration of gardens and low-income housing.

As a trade-off, we may be forced to accept that the city would officially own the garden land, because they are paying to buy it. But we are talking (lawyers again) about how to assure that the city will be bound under the terms of sale to keep the land as open space or gardens" in perpetuity. These things are never sure, but legally it will be as close to forever as we can hope for.

Going to those Neighborhood Council meetings over the years sure worked out. We benefited from the City Council and zoning-plan meetings where we got urban gardens into the "encourage" list. Now we get to tell city planners it's part of the City's plan to support us!

I want to be able to stand on the street overlooking St. Stephen's garden on another moonlit night. I want us to own that garden and farm it without the nagging fear of impending bulldozers. We're working to make that happen. And if we lose that garden, we will save what we can and cry together for our victories and losses.

In the future, what will the Guadalupe Land Trust look like? We imagine a greenbelt of open space; connecting neighbors otherwise separated in the city. Gardeners in our community will feed themselves, their families and others. The gardens can be a source of income for some and of life for all. Community will be seen in soil health: by building and caring for the soil that gives life, we look after the future and preserve the past. We

Gene's garden and the Guadalupe House and mural

want to walk through these gardens together making our present as good as we can, and leaving the earth a better place when we go.

At this stage I don't know how all this legal-system stuff fits with my anti-authoritarian leanings and vaguely anarchist Catholic Worker principles, but we're going ahead with this experiment, in order to preserve as much of the land as we can. We still have four gardens in our neighborhood that we hope to buy. We want to get going on those soon. The tax-exempt status is a pain, but I think it will help us in fundraising to get land. We keep hearing how there's money out there if we are set up to ask for it.

In the future, what will the Guadalupe Land Trust look like? We imagine a greenbelt of open space; connecting neighbors otherwise separated in the city. Gardeners in our community will feed themselves, their families and others. The gardens can be a source of income for some and of life for all.

Collards, Lead and Arson

The Food Project's Pollution Prevention Program

Roxbury, MA

cleo

an interview with Jess Hayes

"While weeding The Food Project's Langdon Street food lot, my attention was drawn to a neighbor's small plot of land, crowded with corn and collards, on the other side of a chain-link fence. Not once, as I kneeled in the dirt, did I stop to think about the lead levels in the soil or what pesticides might have been applied to that corn. Even further from my mind was the thought that the following spring Colleen, Vanusa and I would be on the other side of that fence, in our rain gear, cleaning up that land for the neighboring gardener Dominga.

Trash bag after trash bag bulged with dead plants (it was the corn I had seen the previous growing season) rock after rock was stacked along the borders, and shovelful after shovelful of trash-filled soil was hauled out. A soil test revealed lead levels to be over 1000 parts per million (ppm), a number well over the safety level of 300 ppm. When all was said and done, it seemed miraculous that Dominga's crops has grown so well in such contaminated land. On another level, the realization struck me as incredible that urban gardeners were unaware of the dangers of growing produce in polluted soil."

—Jennifer Miller, The Food Project Pollution Prevention intern

Jess Hayes

There are a lot of environmental justice issues in this community— eight out of the nine Boston waste transfer stations are in Roxbury as well as eight bus depots. The asthma rates in Dudley (a neighborhood in Roxbury) are six times higher than average. Most of the houses were painted with lead paint, before it was banned in the mid 1970s. The paint eventually chips off and ends up in the soil. In an area that was burned the lead goes immediately into the soil. And it just accumulates—it doesn't break down.

incinerator in Roxbury at Jackson Square

drawings by Loren Hellfire

Seventy-five years ago, Dudley was mostly an Italian neighborhood. After World War II a lot of immigrants moved in. Italians and other white people fled to the suburbs, but continued being landowners. By the '60s and '70s it had become primarily an African-American and immigrant community. The landowners could make more money by burning their buildings and collecting insurance than by collecting rent. So they burned. In a sixty acre area they opened up 1300 lots.

In the 80's the Dudley Street Neighborhood Initiative (DSNI) started organizing from within the community to take it back. The organization claimed eminent domain over an area just under a mile square. It was the first community-development group in the country to get the right of eminent domain, and the first to use it for something for other than moving people out to build highways.

Eminent domain gives DSNI the right to decide what happens on any land owned by the city, or any land unclaimed by private property owners within the Dudley Street neighborhood. DSNI has done a lot to revitalize this neighborhood by building new homes, and, through the Food Project, feeding people.

With the youth interns in the Pollution Prevention

Program we mapped out the whole neighborhood and found 168 gardens in this 1 square mile area. We tested the soil and found soil concentrations of lead up to 7000 (ppm). Lead is found naturally in concentrations of around 50 ppm. The US government says that safe levels are under 300 ppm, which I still wouldn't want to grow a lot of food in. Lead contamination in soil comes mostly from paint chips and from lead in fuel.

Lead is a really sticky metal that gets absorbed by living tissues, both plant and animal, very quickly. Garden vegetables readily absorb lead. In an urban area like Dudley, people often grow corn and collards in the strip next to the house, where the lead levels are the highest.

If you eat lead through soil, dust or through plants it attaches to the fatty tissue in your brain. In adult bodies it has been associated with osteoporosis because it will attach to the calcium in your bloodstream and keep it from being absorbed by your bones. In kids it causes serious developmental and neurological problems.

Most gardeners hadn't done soil tests. Some people knew about lead poisoning, but didn't know about the dangers of lead in food. Many weren't literate in English: most of the information available about lead is in English, and it's about kids and paint and not about food production.

The average income in this community is $7400 per person, so there's an economic need for the food that's grown in people's backyards. In addition, studies have shown that food grown organically in urban areas is usually healthier and contains fewer contaminants than vegetables on supermarket shelves. So our challenge was to keep land in food production while finding ways to lower the levels of lead in the soil.

The gardens of Roxbury, MA

Remediating Toxic Soil

Lead wants to bind, so it binds to the organic matter in compost and prevents the plants from taking it up. We've been working with three gardeners, adding two feet of compost to their gardens over the last two years, and it has brought the lead levels down.

To expand this program we're going to need to find a cheaper source of organic material. It's very expensive for an organization to buy compost, but the city could do it very easily. They're making compost from Cambridge yard waste, which they could use in the gardens here in Roxbury.

Another thing we could do is take these gardens out of production for one season to try to remediate the soil. We've also been looking into phytoremediation, which is using non-food plants to absorb lead. You can plant 5 rotations of Indian mustard or sunflowers in a season, which would absorb a lot of the lead out of the soil. You have to treat the plants like toxic waste and get them incinerated or disposed of somewhere else. There are places where they reclaim the lead from the ashes, but incineration of toxic waste is very expensive.

I researched some of the soil remediation options that Jessica discussed on the EPA's website (http://www.epa.gov/opptintr/lead/ is a good place to start). EPA scientists have conducted studies on phytoremediation using mustard plants, but these large-scale trials don't necessarily apply to small-scale urban gardening situations. Jess and I decided that gardeners need to do more research in this field, so that we can develop strategies to transform toxic urban land into productive gardens. Please let us know what you discover!
—cleo

Environmental Justice

Carla Campbell
The Food Project Pollution Prevention Program Intern

While we were mapping, we stopped to survey 16 gardeners and ask them questions such as: "How long have you been gardening?" "Do you know what lead is?" and "Who eats the produce you grow?" We had the help of neighborhood kids to translate when the gardeners didn't speak English. I was really impressed that despite these language difficulties, none of the people got annoyed with us. Instead they were proud to display their gardens and let us take pictures so that we could document the neighborhood.

We have continued working with neighborhood gardener Honario this summer. He's been working with The Food Project for two years so I got to see him go through the whole process of remediating his land: soil testing, spreading mineral-rich compost, installing compost bins in his garden, and picking out any harmful bugs. Honario's been very interested and eager to learn more and more about organic gardening methods and he has gotten to the point where he's able to sell his produce at The Food Project's Thursday Farmer's Market. Now at the market his neighbors stop by and express their surprise that Honario is there, selling his own vegetables, and discussing his practices in his native language of Cape Verdean Creole.

Beyond Garden Plots

Youth Interns took the information they gathered through the Community Mapping project and their work with gardeners to City Hall. What were your goals in meeting with the city?

Carla Campbell: First, we wanted a way for backyard gardeners all over the city to get compost—this would help residents combat high lead levels in soil. Second, we wanted to develop multi-lingual signage to put up around the Roxbury and Dorchester communities in areas with high lead levels to warn people that there is in fact risk involved with growing in those areas. Lastly, when we were mapping out the number of community gardens within Dorchester and Roxbury, we found that in places where there was new housing there wasn't any 'green space.' We wanted there to be some bill or movement that could allocate green space for gardens whenever there was new development.

What are the impacts of the Pollution Prevention Program on the Dudley neighborhood?

It makes people think and that is huge! I hope that it will help people understand that although building a restaurant or houses on a vacant plot of land may mean quicker economic increase, designating the area as green space, whether it be a park or a garden, will mean instant beautification and increased community productiveness. I know this is true because I have talked to residents near The Food Project's West Cottage Lot in Dorchester. They appreciate our garden and watch over it when we are not there. Our work also makes people aware of the dangers of lead in the soil and what they can do to solve this problem.

The gardeners we work with are examples of what's possible when people put their minds to caring for the land.

Pollution Prevention interns with Joe, adding compost to his Roxbury garden.

Youth cultivate The Food Project's Langdon St. lot

photos courtesy of The Food Project

Urban-Rural Connections

papercut by Tiffany

The Victory Gardens Project: Athens, ME; Boston, MA; New York, NY; Newark & East Orange, NJ

Ha:san Preparatory and Leadership Academy: Tucson and Wa:k, AZ

"Continuous, sprawling urbanization destroys life, and makes cities unbearable....With the breakdown of contact between city dwellers and the countryside, the cities become prisons."

— *A Pattern Language,* "City-Country Fingers"

Along the coasts of North America, cities drop dots on maps of huge open space. They gather in clusters blurring into a megalopolis containing hundreds of millions of people. In the middle of the country the dots drop between fields of soy and corn. Between these cities, vast expanses of open space push the horizon. On the prairies and plains, wheat and corn, soybeans and canola, potatoes and sugar beets fill thousands of acres of space. In the arid west, cows graze millions of acres of public land, polluting groundwater, causing widespread erosion and the displacement of wild predators. In other areas, forest-farms of hybrid and genetically engineered trees are clearcut for pulp and export lumber. This is the heartland, 'feeding people everywhere.' However, little of this land grows food for people. Most is monoculture fields of animal feed or products that are refined into commodities.

On the surface, city landscapes look very different from the expanses of grain and beans that stretch through the middle of the continent. But just as the monoculture of plants is not grown to feed people, neither is the space in cities dedicated to meeting the daily needs of the people who live there. Road space accounts for more than 50% of urban land. There are tall buildings, banks, restaurants, insurance companies, investment corporations, a myriad assortment of offices that 'house people making money' while other people hunger for space in which to live— not simply shelter at night, but space in which to interact, grow and discover.

In ecology, 'edge' refers to the space where two different ecosystems meet. This could be a forest and a prairie, or river and desert, At the place where differences meet, life thrives. New species and relationships develop. The dynamics of cities work on this same principle of 'edge', but here it is not an ecological but a cultural edge; plants and animals find relationships with each other that never happen in their indigenous environments, and humans find ways of mixing language, food, music, games and religion.

So while cities and rural places look different to the eye, what's actually going on in both is similar There are endless possibilities for dynamic, thriving habitats for life. Unfortunately, what is also similar about these environments is that much of rural and urban space is used to serve commerce alone. It's the same theme in a different form. Agriculture directly connects urban and rural people, land and economies together.

—Andrea del Moral, from "Seeds in the City"

For us cityfolk, rural farms provide a much larger land base to grow food on, and an escape from the fast pace of the city. At the Victory Gardens Project in Athens, ME, urban and rural people work together growing food for both the local rural community and New Afrikan organizations in the city. As political prisoner and Victory Gardens member Jalil Muntaqim says, "the Victory Gardens project is not just about growing veggies." Rather, the food that is grown here is a revolutionary tool that brings people together to form a new society inside the present one.

At Ha:sañ, a charter school for Native American high school students in Tucson, AZ, the ethnobotanical garden adapts the traditional desert gardening practices of the Tohono O'odham to an urban setting. After working in the garden at Ha:sañ, many students begin cultivating traditional crops in their villages on the res, reviving agricultural methods that were severely threatened by government programs in the early part of this century.

As Andrea points out, the diversity and vibrance of both urban and rural cultures are threatened by monoculture, resource extraction and commerce. Urban-rural connections create new ways to bring life back to the city and thecountryside.

Free the Land! The Victory Gardens Project

Errol Schweizer
MayDay 2001

Flashback to October 20, 2000. It was autumn and the leaves were changing. I'm standing outside Mrs. Jackson's house in East Orange, NJ, headquarters of the Uhuru Organization, a local group that does youth mentoring and organizing in the community. The block is electric. People are dancing, playing drums and rhyming into the mic about Black liberation and self-determination. The lawn of Mrs. Jackson's house is covered with brown paper shopping bags, overflowing with fresh produce and colorfully stenciled with messages: *"Free Mumia!" "Free The NY3!" "Free All Political Prisoners!"* The organic, hand-picked produce—potatoes, garlic, squash, cilantro, carrots—is grown by volunteers on a farm in Maine.

The event is the annual food distribution of the Victory Gardens Project, an organizing collaboration between inner city and rural community groups.

Founded in 1996 by New York 3 (NY 3) Afrikan Liberation prisoner Herman Bell and working class environmentalists Carol Dove and Michael Vernon, the Victory Gardens Project (VGP) is attempting to bridge the divide between oppressed urban and rural communities, while merging the struggles for black liberation and earth liberation; as Malcolm X once pointed out, all revolutionary struggles are centered on the question of land.

The VGP was inspired equally by the survival programs of the Black Panther Party, of which the NY 3 were a part, and the nature-based philosophy of the radical ecology and anarchist movements. In 1994, Carol and Michael started to support the MOVE organization in Philadelphia by bringing them fresh, organic food from their garden in Maine. At the suggestion of Herman Bell, the VGP was expanded to include bringing food to inner-city community groups, as well as bringing volunteers up from these urban communities, such as Uhuru members from East Orange, to work on the garden.

Volunteers are the backbone of the project. They come up to Athens, Maine and experience a world far different from urban life. The homestead is two miles down a rocky dirt road on thickly wooded land, over the hill from a deep blue pond. Over five miles from the closest power line, electricity is generated by solar power, water is pumped from a well and meals are cooked from food grown on-site or bought in bulk. The project is structured collectively and without a hierarchy so that everyone can participate, contribute and resolve conflicts easier. This is especially important since VGP is attempting to bridge the class and race gaps in radical politics.

from a VGP educational pamphlet

Herman Bell, who is locked down at Clinton Correctional Facility in Dannemora, New York, says that the VGP is based on the idea that only through collective self help can people improve their material conditions. It is an extension of the survival programs started by the Black Panther Party in the 1960s, which asserted that communities could organize to take care of their own needs, such as jobs, food, housing, health care, and education. In terms of independent food production, VGP shows how much food can be produced by

"The Victory Gardens is not just about growing veggies."
— Jalil Muntaqim, NY 3 Political Prisoner

committed volunteers; with three parcels of land totaling well under two acres (or a little bigger than a football field), they grew over 12,000 pounds of food last summer, including carrots, potatoes, squash, peas, corn, beans, spinach, cilantro and garlic. Most of the food was delivered to communities in Massachusetts, New Jersey and New York, although a great deal of food was also distributed locally in Maine.

The VGP also works with political prisoners in order to increase support for their clemency/amnesty campaigns. The project encourages volunteers to correspond with political prisoners and make trips to visit jailed revolutionaries. The NY 3 martyr Albert "Nuh" Washington was an avid victory gardener and NY 3 member Jalil Muntaqim contributes many ideas to the project. And if a group wants to be involved in the food distribution, they must first contact Herman Bell.

The project is an organic, evolving process that is based on putting revolutionary ideas into practice. Jalil explains:"the road to revolution is a process and not an event, and we all must be about the process of revolution."

The VGP is a model for community organizing; volunteers not only share their labor and ideas on the farm, but they then go back to their own communities where they develop these ideas and get community members talking and working together. VGP not only supports community organizing in urban areas, but also organizes their own community by sharing food, encouraging cooperative labor and alternatives to the cash-based economy, as well as giving out information on political prisoners, the prison-industrial complex and living a healthy life.

VGP also bridges the gap between rural and urban communities that would otherwise not have much contact with each other. The key to understanding globalization, poverty and the prison boom is by looking at both rural and urban areas. Urban people of color fill the prisons which are built in rural areas. Carol, who grew up in rural Maine, says, "because of globalization, rural areas have been scoped out for prison construction because the better jobs are gone and people have to get service industry work. Their self esteem drops, their integrity is diminished. The system sets up barriers for low-income people to battle amongst themselves. But if people rose up against the system and supported each other, the system would fall."

The Victory Gardens Project is also building an alternative to corporate control of the food supply. "Agribusiness is centralized power that can only be done under a system that exploits from the top down. It exploits the earth and enslaves the people who consume the food and work for the production of the food. It is dependent on heavy machinery, fossil fuels, and bigger equipment that means more bankers are involved and more debt," says Michael, a former migrant laborer.

Considering over 80% of processed food is genetically modified, most poor people, especially in the inner cities, have little access to healthy, organic food. Food production under capitalism is therefore racist and classist; mostly wealthier people have access to healthy, natural food. Meanwhile, poor neighborhoods have liquor stores, KFCs and Mickey Ds. It makes sense to have alternatives that enable low-income people and people of color to eat healthy, preventing the heart disease, asthma and cancer that follow poverty.

VGP members think that the way Wall Street maintains loyalty to this system is through consumerism, which creates apathy. According to Carol, "When people are working meaningless jobs and have no reason for living other than making money, they got to have some glossy or high-tech gratification." Cristina Adamo, a core group member of the project, points out that "the instant gratification keeps people distracted from real problems."

The VGP also articulates a vision of liberation that creates independence from the global economy. "I really see that freedom is connected to responsibility. If you want to be free then you have to be responsible for

Victory Gardens core group members Cristina Adamo and Carol Dove view poster of martyred NY3 Political Prisoner, former member of the Black Panther Party and Black Liberation Army, Albert Nuh Washington, who died alone in prison on April 28, 2000, from liver cancer, after 29 years behind the walls. This poster, resting above the food distribution bags, contains a poem for Nuh by VG volunteer Richard Cambridge. Nuh participated in the Victory Gardens Project along with NY3 political prisoners Jalil Muntaqim and Herman Bell. In fact, Nuh was a Victory Gardener who maintained a small veggie patch, with seeds he received from our project, in the honor block of Clinton prison. Nuh shared his produce with the other prisoners he was housed with. Nuh continually shared his courage, strength, sage wisdom, sharp wit, and generous love with us all. We continue to honor his memory. —Herman Bell

Clockwise from top: 2000 harvest; distribution in East Orange,
Michael explains the Athens farm; carrot harvest; Kazi Touré

yourself and your surroundings. So I would challenge people who are technophiles to be responsible for their daily needs. They're not producing their own food, they're not producing their own shelter, they're not producing their own clothing, they're not taking responsibility for the education of themselves and their children, they're not taking responsibility for their own health. And taking responsibility for those things, although it's really difficult in a lot of different ways, is liberating and it's hard to imagine an argument for liberation and freedom that doesn't include those things," explains Michael.

The Victory Gardens Project shows that the havoc created by globalization can stopped in a practical way on a community-based level. From downtown East Orange, to the backwoods of Maine, and on to the jungles of Chiapas and slums of São Paolo, people throughout the world are losing their livelihoods and are forced to become dependent on a system that imprisons, starves, tortures and kills them for the sake of profit. If we are going to build a real alternative to capitalism, then we can no longer be dependent on it to provide basic needs. Instead, we need to build a network of self-sufficient communities who will work together and trust and educate each other to survive the coming struggles.

Or as Carol says, "Its all about hope. Hope is a big thing."

Radical Rural Organizing

at the Ray Space in Athens, ME

Athens, Maine, a rural and impoverished community, is home to the Victory Gardens project. The Athens community is involved in the project from the beginning. Farmers and community members donate land in the middle of town, accessible to the many young people and town members who help maintain the project. Community members benefit and support the project in many ways. Some people exchange vegetables for eggs or labor and machinery for hay. Seed sharing occurs through seed giveaways in the spring. People work together to find shoes for the kids' growing feet, clothing for whoever needs it and hay to insulate homes through the winter, all through the existence of the VGP.

Resources are abundant within this self-sufficient style of organizing. Everything is used and nothing is wasted. During the harvest, carrot tops are saved for horses— the owner of those horses helps transport the harvested tons of carrots to be washed and boxed. The beet greens are saved for the cows of the neighboring farm, and the vegetables are distributed throughout both the local town and in cities hundreds of miles away.

The use of hay in the gardens is a clear example of natural resources being used to their fullest potential. Hay grows at the land where most of the vegetables are produced. A neighboring dairy farmer bales the hay for the project, keeping half for his cows as payment. The other half is sold in town by the farmer who owns the land. In the winter, hay is used to insulate houses. In the spring when the hay is soaked and muddied, Victory Gardeners travel through town gathering this dirty hay to use as compost for the newly planted garden beds. Nothing is wasted. Everyone benefits.

During the winter the VGP offers a variety of community-building events. Victory Gardeners make it clear that the project is not about charity. instead, the VGP draws on resources within the community to provide clothing, food and other basic needs for free. Free Movie Fridays include both film screenings, discussions, and presentations local Athens history, and are attended by filled-room audiences. Free Soup Sundays provide a space to build community locally while informing the townspeople about the broader goals of the project.

Local distributions of food occur daily throughout the fall in Athens. There are two distribution sites where freshly picked food is laid out for anyone to come pick up. Signs declare the goals of the project and how to get involved. A variety of food is put out: pickling cucumbers, dill, fresh flowers, purple string beans, and Mainer's favorite kind of squash— buttercup. There are signs that the notion of free (and not charity) is catching on around town. Different vegetables have appeared from other folks' gardens. Once, several bikes were left at the tables, with another "Free" sign placed next to them.

Support for US Political Prisoners

The VGP draws volunteers from across the country who are interested in learning sustainable farming techniques. Volunteers walk away with much more than gardening lessons. Through films, letters from prisoners and prison visits, volunteers are exposed to the cases, current conditions, history of social movements, and the resistance of freedom fighters in the US. Many volunteers from the project create ongoing relationships with political prisoners after their time at the VGP, others write letters in support of specific action alerts on behalf of prisoners, and still others are introduced for the first time to the connections between the freeing of the land through sustainable agriculture and liberation for all people. Through active support, education, skills sharing, meeting basic needs, providing organic food, sharing resources, and fighting all forms of oppression, the VGP makes connections that serve as a model to creating the building blocks we need as we fight together for a new society. —Sonja Sveisend

Feed a Village

cleo

an interview with Farmer Dave and Ha:sañ students

I pilot the borrowed green 3-speed down the wide, dusty streets of Tucson, Arizona's university district, looking for a food garden among the palms, oleanders and cactus that dominate the gravel yards of this sprawling urban neighborhood. I'm looking for Farmer Dave, who runs the ethnobotany program at Ha:sañ (pronounced *ha shan*) Preparatory and Leadership School, a charter high school for Tohono O'odham and other Native American youth. I come around the corner and see sunken beds of peas, onions and greens, long windrows of compost, and piles of mulch. The school used to be a Presbyterian church, with a huge parking lot and a lawn in front. Now, traditional crops grow where the lawn and parking lot used to be, and students have planted native trees to shade what asphalt remains.The permaculture and ethnobotany classes have also built straw-bale cold frames and a traditional outdoor kitchen.

When I walk into Farmer's classroom, the first thing I notice are squash as big as a small child, as well as corn and gourds drying on a table. These are all traditional crops of the Tohono O'odham, which the students have grown for seed. Over the next few days, Farmer gives me some background information on the project, while the students talk about the role of the urban garden in the school, the neighborhood, and their villages.

What is unique about the garden project at Ha:sañ?

The whole project at Ha:sañ is built upon the foundation of knowledge that underlies Native American farming and gardening methods in the Southwest. Twenty-two nations scattered across Arizona, California, Chihuahua, Durango, New Mexico, Sinaloa and Sonora selected varieties of crops able to withstand long drought, intense heat, high elevations and alkaline soil conditions. If we were to tour the scattered garden plots of canyons, mesas, mountain slopes and riverbanks in the Southwest we could see firsthand the tremendous diversity of crops developed by First Nations: blue-speckled beans from 8000 feet, a chocolate-colored sweet chile, maize varieties that can be planted several feet below the surface to avoid drought, squash whose shells can be made into musical instruments, a black-seeded sunflower used for dye, a red-seeded watermelon, a white maize flecked with blue like a robin's egg. I flipped through a seed catalog from Native Seed/SEARCH, a Tucson-based seed conservatory of First Nations crops and counted 12 amaranth, 34 bean, 24 chile, 69 maize, 14 gourd, 29 melon and 37 squash varieties.

Sopol Esabig Masad (Short Planting Season Moon)

Swales were used by the Mogollon Culture in Arizona in AD 700. Swales are raised berms of dirt or rocks built along contour lines that capture surface runoff. The swale snaking through the right half of the photo was built by Ha:san students in village of Wa:k. Note soil darkened by moisture toward the swale.

The stakes and birdnetting were set up to protect the crops from ground squirrels (*chehkol*) which are numerous and decimated some of the crops. If you look at the lower left corner of the garden bed you can see a whitish line extending parallel to the stake. This is the real tragedy of th bird netting—it kills snakes. That white line is the upper portion of a four-foot long coach-whip snake (*chuk wamaD*), the third snake to have died in the netting (two coach-whips and a gopher snake (*Sho'owa*). A red racer (*wegi wamaD*) and a coach-whip were released stressed but unharmed. Still, too many dead snakes for my tastes.

photos this article by Farmer Dave

69

Store Water in the Soil with Swales!

Desert gardeners have long used water-harvesting structures called swales to store water in the soil. Dug on the contours of the land, swales help stop erosion and provide water to garden plants and plants used in land restoration.

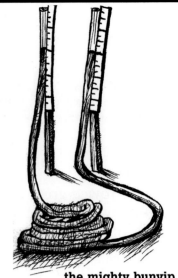

drawings by Greg Jalbert

View of a tool known as a bunyip or carpenter's level. Basically, it is a clear plastic tube filled with water and attached to a pair of poles that have rulers on them. The tool is used to find locations of equal elevation so that water-harvesting features (swales) can be laid out.

the mighty bunyip

The students use the bunyip tool to find the contour of the land. The contour lines are marked and a berm (swale) is built on these lines. By building a berm of soil on contour the thin layer of water that runs across the soil after a rain (sheet runoff) can be harvested. Swales built by the Mogollon culture between A.D.1000 and 1430 can be found at Point of Pines, AZ.

Plan view of a series of swales. The black lines are contour lines; gray areas represent water stopped behind the swales. The top of the slope is in the bottom left corner of the illustration.

When it rains the sheet runoff runs downslope, hits the swale and stops. This allows the sheet runoff to infiltrate into the soil, directly in the root zone of trees or crops planted in the berm. Much like the ancient O'odham we are trying to trap nutrients and increase the water retention capacity of the soil.

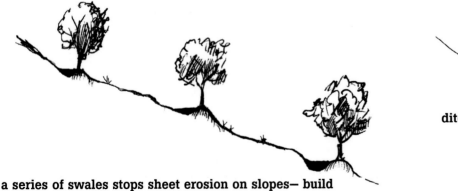

a series of swales stops sheet erosion on slopes— build swales on gentle slopes (less than 15%)

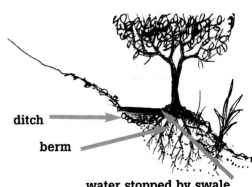

ditch

berm

water stopped by swale

The Tohono O'odham ("desert people") dry farmed in some of the hottest, driest regions of North America. In their part of the Sonoran Desert annual rainfall averages less than five inches while temperatures exceed 100 degrees for five months of the year. Yet the O'odham selected a cushaw-type of squash (*ha:l*) that thrived on runoff, an extremely fast-growing maize (*huhni*) variety that beats the heat by maturing in sixty days, a bean called tepary bean (*w'pegi bawi*) that tolerates soil surface temperatures of 130 degrees, and a plant, devil's claw (*ihug*), whose multiple uses include: seeds rich in oil and protein, fruits eaten like okra and fibers used in coiled baskets.

For urban gardeners and *permaculturistas* the traditional gardening methods of the Tohono O'odham are an inspiration. To supplement their diet of wild plants and hunted animals they grew fifteen varieties of cultivated crops using only surface runoff from the short, intense, widely-scattered thunderstorms of the summer monsoon which occur from late June to early September. A series of brush dams were placed on the flats and washes of the valley floor to slow sheet runoff from adjacent mountains. The runoff then soaked deep into the soil, dumping its load of debris. This debris consists of silt and nitrogen-rich leaves of mesquite, palo verde and ironwood trees, which added fertility to the O'odham fields.

Al Ju:Big Masad (Small Rains Moon- October)

Hu:n (60-day corn) *wakona* (dipper gourds) and *ha:l* (cushaw squash)— some of the traditional Tohono O'odham crops vital to preserve the culture and health of our students

A variation of this method was even used in the Pinacate— a section of the Sonoran Desert that sees rain only once every few years. At a site known as Suvuk a group of Tohono O'odham, the Sand People or Hiach-eD O'odham, planted maize (*huhni*), beans (*w'pegi bawi*) and squash (*ha:l*) in a bowl of volcanic rock less than five acres and filled with soil. Other than the odd year when the Hiach-eD O'odham would spot the telltale cloud over Suvuk that sent them rushing to plant, the Sand People were strictly hunter-gatherers.

All this is to say that the Tohono O'odham were excellent gardeners. Yet government programs such as federally-constructed wells and provisional foods effectively ended their traditional lifestyle. Between 1919 and 1980 floodwater fields (*oidag*) decreased from 16,000 acres to less than 100 acres. Loss of the oidag was accompanied by the disappearance of seasonal villages and the gathering of wild plant foods as the basis of their nutrition.

What are some of the ongoing effects of the government's destruction of traditional O'odham livelihood?

Challenges facing Tohono O'odham youth include high rates of non-insulin dependent diabetes, attributed to the change from wild plant and animal foods, and a disruption of traditional agricultural and botanical knowledge. Because this knowledge provides a tie to the landscape within which the O'odham live, it provides the identity of their being. The loss of this intimate connection to the landscape experienced by land-based cultures is referred to by anthropologists as an "extinction of experience". This refers to a form of alienation that accompanies the rapid cultural losses that the O'odham and other First Nations people were subjected to by the United States government; symptoms include low self-esteem, depression, alcoholism, irreconcilable anger and suicide.

Against this backdrop, the Ha:sañ Service Learning Program in 2000 developed a garden at a community center in the Tohono O'odham Village of Wa:k (San Xavier). In constructing the garden beds there, Tohono O'odham youth used permaculture techniques to harvest surface runoff much as their ancestors did. High-school and middle school students, community center employees and a few elders harvested ocotillo (*melhog*) for a traditional living fence to encircle the garden and then prepared and planted the beds. One day, the librarian at the community center saw someone rescuing a coachwhip snake (*chuk wamaD*) that had gotten tangled in the bird-netting in the garden. As she watched him gently untangle the snake it made her think what her grandmother had taught her about how you were supposed to be nice to snakes. For the librarian, the garden initially retrieved a cultural memory in the form of a story and then seemed to reinforce the positive feelings she got from that memory which in her words were "that every little life is important."

So the program is about much more than just growing plants?

In addition to the physical work of digging beds and starting seeds, Ha:sañ garden students visit urban gardens, seed farms, botanical gardens, permaculture proj-

71

ects, and participate in cultural events such as the Desert Walk. The Desert Walk was a 280 mile walk across the Sonoran Desert to educate the public about wild and traditionally cultivated plant foods. It also raised awareness of the diabetes epidemic striking First Nation peoples. Approximately 50 Comcaa'c (Seri) and Tohono O'odham (including four Ha:sañ students) took part in the journey across desert basins and mountains.

The current year's project focused on laying the foundation for the garden at Ha:sañ with fruit trees, native shrubs and trees, pollinator gardens and an outdoor kitchen. The transformation of the schoolground landscape away from an inedible monoculture (bermuda grass and asphalt) to trees (fig, citrus, mesquite, pomegranate, ironwood, palo verde) and other plants (prickly pear, cholla cactus, desert hackberry, agave, wolfberry, traditional crops) creates a living classroom that provide cultural and nutritional tools to quell the diabetes epidemic amongst the Tohono O'odham.

What are some of the benefits of this type of garden in an urban landscape?

As Tucson sprawls in all directions a very diverse native Sonoran Desert flora and fauna is replaced by asphalt, houses, swimming pools and a reduced flora of non-native plants from around the world. The roads, buildings and parking lots store the heat of a summer's day and take much longer to cool at night than the natural desert. This heat changes local climate by evaporating evening storm clouds and decreasing the number of nighttime thunderstorms. The more radical architects and planners have called for asphalt removal as a way to begin to heal this phenomenon of the desert called the urban heat island effect. Through the implementation of their permaculture design the students at Ha:sañ have cut the size of the school's parking lot by one third, replacing the missing asphalt with garden space and tree wells.

Worldwide there has been an alarming drop in pollinator populations— bats, moths, butterflies, wasps and bees. Because plants and animals have coevolved with insects, many have highly-developed relationships and are therefore susceptible to decreases in pollinator populations. For example, saguaro cactus (*Ha:sañ*) also provides pollen for the bat which is its main pollinator. As pollinator habitat is lost and native pollinator populations decline, biologists have observed lower seed set in both rare plants and commercial crops. Straight up: no pollinators=no seed; no seed=no food. Tucson area schools are participating with pollination biologists at the Arizona-Sonoran Desert Museum to plant gardens that provide food for migrating pollinators.

The neighborhood where Ha:sañ is located has long been a target of the nearby university's attempts to use eminent domain for expansion. Local residents have often felt ignored and disempowered when compared to other wealthier, more powerful neighborhoods

San Xavier Education Center, Wa:k, AZ

Ocotillo (*melhog*) is a type of succulent that has been used traditionally by the Tohono O'odham as a building material. To make a living fence, cuttings are placed in a trench in the ground between mesquite posts secured with baling wire and various styles of cross-pieces. The ocotillo for the garden fence was harvested on the very far southwestern part of the reservation and brought to the Wa:k education center in the back of a trailer. Middle school students helped cut and carry the live ocotillo poles.

top: some students devised ingenious ways to carry the thorny ocotillo

bottom: the nearly-completed fence around the garden at Wa:k

around the university who have been successful in resisting their expansion. The presence of a garden in a struggling neighborhood can be a wellspring for building pride and self-esteem. The outdoor kitchen serves as a meeting place for both the neighborhood residents and the parents of Ha:sañ students. Not only can students learn the Tohono O'odham names for plants but non-O'odham folks can too. Having the means to prepare meals in the garden completes the cycle of food growing taking place in the urban garden at Ha:sañ.

Farmer Dave and his 3rd period class give us a tour of the Ha:sañ garden

Farmer: These are special onions from the res, they're called *I'itoi*. How can you best describe *I'itoi*?

Student: He's an O'odham guy—he's the creator.

Farmer: The onions regenerate, they clone. I think that's why they named them *I'itoi's*. They can dry up, and then be stuck back in the ground. They're a bunching onion, so you plant a few and suddenly there's tons of them, and you can split those.

This garden is sheet-mulched with layers of bark and manure. The bark is from this cordwood place. It's all mesquite bark which is very high in nitrogen. The top layer is compost the class made using produce trimmings, manure and soil. We plant in the top layer of compost. The whole thing is about three feet thick. And things are doing really good in here. We planted heavy feeders here in the springtime.

All these mustards are from tribes in Mexico. Those are O'odham peas. Most of the stuff we try to grow is culturally relevant. Some of it isn't, but in the traditional winter gardens they didn't grow as much, and most of it came from the Spanish anyway. The peas and garbanzos did.

Most of the summer garden is planted in O'odham crops, but there are students from other tribes in the class as well. There are Dine', there's people who are Mojave and O'odham, Hopi and O'odham, Mexican and O'odham, so we try to grow stuff that applies to everybody.

At times the aesthetics of a food-producing garden clash with people's perceptions of how a schoolyard is supposed to look. One student commented, "Why should we clean up? This is how we are. We should be proud of it. So what if there's a big pile of cement that we haven't moved out yet." The site is in constant transformation.

There's one person in particular who wants to put a fence around the garden to hide it, because when there's nothing growing, these beds are "unsightly". What's unsightly about seeing earth instead of clean cement?

Sopol Esabig Masad (Short Planting Season Moon)

Flowers watered with runoff from the courtyard & fertilized with bat guano, fish emulsion, greensand & phosphate at Ha:san

Ha:sañ student Reynaldo Preston answers some questions

How does the garden get watered?

These guys water it once in a while. Farmer doesn't water it when it rains. The courtyard's on a hill, so all the water runs into the beds when it rains.

I remember coming down here one time in the summer and the plants were really big. We grew corn, beans, cabbage, lettuce, squash.

The squash plants grew all the way up the railings to the door handles. This whole place was covered with squash plants. It's an O'odham squash. It's called *ha:l* (pronounced *harrr*—the r is rolled like in Spanish)

We took some of the food to the camp and cooked it, when we went to Richard's seed farm in the Gila.

I like tomatoes. I grew some for a while when I was smaller.

Did you grow anything else when you were little?

My grandpa had a plot. I don't know what he planted. He still has the land but he doesn't plant anymore.

Is anyone from your family going to take that over?

My cousin probably will. I was thinking about putting some gardens behind my house out on the res.

Why do think it's important to grow food?

To save money, and to preserve our food and our culture.

Your people developed some pretty impressive plants. Those squashes were amazing. We europeans developed all these delicate little herbs.

We have to feed a village. That's serious.

Harrison Preston, another student of Farmer's, talks about growing traditional crops

Have you ever gardened before?

Last year I started my own garden at my house. It was my first time so I grew devil's claw and gourds.

What did you do with the devil's claw?

I use them. I do basketry. The gourds are still drying.

What made you want to start gardening?

Lack of materials. I did it so I could have more to work with.

Do you grow basketry materials here as well?

No, they need the summer monsoons to get longer, so I'm just going to grow them this summer at my house.

So what's the advantage of having a garden in the city?

Inner-city people don't grow things much. Out of the city you have the freedom to do a lot more. But the garden here can be a tool to reach a lot of people.

O'odham Crops: an interview with Derek Redhorn, a former student of Farmer Dave's

Tell me about the desert walk.

We just walked. We ate some good foods though. Cholla buds, chiles, onions, squash, tepary beans, roasted rabbit, wild greens, corn soup we call *gaisa*. We ate oregon pipe cactus jam, prickly pear juice.

Do you grow any of that here?

The corn, squash, the beans, mainly that stuff. We get the beans from Native Seed/SEARCH. They call the seed by the name of the tribe— O'odham black-eye beans or O'odham pink beans. My favorite is *bah*, that's a white tepary bean. They're rich, kind of creamy.

I have a garden at my house on the res, where I grow O'odham stuff. Corn, beans, stuff like that. After I first learned about growing food here, I made the garden at my house. I still didn't know how to grow, or plant, or harvest, but I always asked my grandmas to help me. They help me a lot.

What's the main difference between your garden on the res and the garden here at the school?

They have more workers here. I grow mainly O'odham, and they grow stuff from lots of different tribes.

What's your favorite thing about the garden here?

You don't see much growing around here. We just

planted out front, and people walk by and they see that, and I think that's good, that they see what we're doing. It's also good that it's the tribe that's making that change, that it's indigenous people who are bringing those plants back. We grow O'odham and crops from other tribes. I do see some people from the neighborhood come by, but it's mostly people from the school.

We have problems growing in the city because the soil's hard, it has a lot of caliche [a hard subsurface layer of calcium and sodium salts common in desert soils]. But we have problems on the res too, like cows. I always told my family, "Keep the gate closed," and one time they didn't and the cows got in and ate my corn. They didn't eat all of it, just pieces of it.

Tell me about the garden on the res.

U'us Wihog Dag Masad (Mesquite Bean Moon)

Intensive planting such as the French biointensive method can be used for growing food in confined areas like urban lots. The gardens at Ha:san show off urban agriculture to the surrounding urban neighborhood.

My brother and I are about the only people that plant over there. There's one other person who plants, down the road, but they plant [non O'odham] things too. We're just planting traditional crops.

Are there many young people who plant?

I think me and my brother are about the only ones. It's really cool because people see us and they ask us, "How's your garden?" and they tell us how much they used to garden. My neighbor, she's always saying that.

Do you think that other kids will get interested in gardening from seeing you do it?

I think people are too interested in urban stuff, like basketball, getting high.

Farmer Dave interjects: He plays in a chicken-scratch band, traditional O'odham music.

I play different instruments, the drums, the guitar, this other instrument called a baho sexto, a mexican guitar. We have a new CD coming out in a couple months.

What advice you would give to other urban gardeners?

The best way is keep on working. You're going to get tired from it, but just keep on doing it. You'll see what you get, and what you get brings so much encouragement that you'll do it over and over.

Compost City:

practical strategies for a free and just world

© Eric Drooker (www.Drooker.com)

London, UK; Washington, D.C.; Oakland, CA; Tucson, AZ; New York, NY; Ljubjana, Slovenia and undisclosed locations in a city near you

"We are Nature, long have we been absent, but now we return."

—Walt Whitman

In North America, it will take a revolution create the cities that gardeners and community activists around the world imagine. This revolution will tear up most of the streets and turn them into food forests and gardens. It will make all vacant land and rooftops available to gardeners. It will replace power plants with rooftop solar panels, blow up dams and build rain-catchment tanks, shut down sewage treatment plants and replace them with wastewater treatment wetlands. It will employ everyone in the massive task of restoring poisoned land, growing food, building healthy housing and creating industries that support human needs without depleting the earth's resources.

At times it's hard to imagine how we'll get from here to there. Capitalism grinds on, in a mechanized orgy of destruction. Acre by acre, suburbs swallow farmland and the wilds disappear under bulldozers, chainsaws, and oil rigs. Our best projects become targets for co-optation. Developers' eyes light up with visions of condos built on community gardens that have brought up property values in formerly burnt out neighborhoods. These same community gardens bring people together, out of their houses and apartment buildings and in off the street corners to plant, harvest and organize.

When I put my ear to the ground, I hear the whispers and rumbles of change taking place, in values and in the world at large. Thousands of kids plant their first seed in gardens at school, take a field trip to a local scrap of wild land to plant forage for birds and butterflies. Many raise their voices in city planning meetings, using their experience of asthma and urban life to demand a different future. Many have come together around the Environmental Justice movement. This movement was born in 1991 at a summit of people of color who asserted that all people have the right to clean air and water, healthy food and shelter, education, employment and the right to live in neighborhoods free of toxic waste. This merging of environmental and social justice concerns was an important step. To take this struggle to the next level we need to assert that a viable world, with free,

76

clean air and water, food and shelter, as well as wild open space, is the most basic right of humans and all living things. Bring nature back into the city and restore the land presently farmed, mined logged and grazed to death so that wild creatures can have space as well. Aside from the intrinsic value of wild places, their effects on human health are direct and clear: forests filter air and create rain, wetlands clean air and water. Beyond the artificial dichotomy of social and environmental issues— loggers' jobs vs. forest habitat, jobs on the industrial waterfront versus the health of the bay and the people who live nearby—there are larger solutions that demand equity and justice while restoring the natural world. As people work—block by block and city by city—to create these solutions, revolution slowly but surely takes root.

It will take a different kind of revolution within agriculture itself to bring farming back into the realm of nature. The best set of tools for that transformation is found within the body of knowledge known as permaculture. Permaculture, a system of design based on traditional indigenous agricultural knowledge, wasdeveloped in Australia in the late 1970s. It contains many on-the-ground tactics for creating a sustainable human culture based on permanent agriculture. More than a collection of gardening techniques, permaculture design models the complex interactions of sun, wind, water, plants and animals that give natural systems their productivity. This concept of "patterning" applies equally to a patio garden and an entire city. Permaculture principles arise from the observation that natural systems are regenerative. When we work with natural processes, we unleash the earth's potential to regenerate.

One ethic of permaculture arises from the following common sense observation: that the earth is bountiful, and that human survival depends on the health of natural ecosystems, so we need to empower people to care for the earth. Without forests and oceans, we have no air to breathe. Without clean water and soil, we can only produce food from fossil fuels for a short time, technophiles' pipe dreams aside. As scientists play with the genetic building blocks of life itself, we have no idea how to contain the long-term effects of releasing genetically modified organisms into the infinetly complex web of biological interactions.

In order to care for the earth, we must create a society that recognizes the connection between human and environmental health, that creates full employment through green technologies and earth repair, and that raises young people to understand and value the natural world. So comes another permaculture ethic: that we must give equal priority to caring for the earth and for people. The ultimate goal is to return human society to the position it once held as one thread in the web of life.

Natural systems aren't greedy. They produce more than they consume and spread the extra around. Design the systems that produce food, timber and fuel for human settlements based on natural models, and they'll generate a surplus. A third permaculture ethic directs us to distribute that surplus for the good of the humans, plants and animals that depend on that system, and to restore the land that this intensive agriculture frees up to wilderness.

At the heart of many permaculture principles is a philosophy of freedom, autonomy and mutual aid. Unfortunately, the permaculture movement in the US has been dominated by those who can afford the courses—mostly white, privileged people with a corresponding lack of investment in social change. When the authors of this anthology talk about permaculture, we mean tools for urban liberation and survival. In our gardens we plant food to give away, not just for ourselves or to sell in upscale farmers' markets, and we plant some for the birds, worms and animals. We act to take responsibility for our basic needs in order to foster independence from a multinational economy driven by fossil fuels, "green revolution" monoculture and inhuman living and working conditions for people that make the products we consume.

It's a long way from the litany of destruction droning on in the news to actually creating sustainable cities. Along the way, we need to create small good things sustain ourselves, to give us hope and space to breathe.

Guerrilla Gardening

primal seeds and anonymous gardeners

...an urban adventure at the threshold of nature and culture, taking back our own time and space, transforming the urban desert into a provider of food and a space where people meet face to face to discuss and participate directly in the remaking of their own towns and cities.

Learning to produce our own food is essential if we are to ever truly take control of our own lives. It liberates us from the role of passive consumer, remote from real decisions, alienated from nature. It is a step away from the grip of capitalism and the concrete boot on the foot of life.

Growing food requires land. Look around you. It's everywhere. If not horizontal, it's vertical. Your imagination is the limit: railway embankments, back gardens, golf courses, roofs, car parks, overgrown bits, cracks in the pavement. The flower beds in your town centre could be growing your crops, right in the heart of the consumer landscape of burger bars, chain stores and supermarkets.

Guerrilla gardeners are out there now. Why not join them in digging for revolution?

Guerrilla Gardening History

So where did it all come from? This movement was born of fanatical gardeners during the 1970s, people who felt themselves unconstrained by such things as property lines and defined space, who sought to beautify or alter the world at random. In the early days, guerrilla gardening was primarily a means of protest. Pot plants would sprout up between petunias in front of police stations and federal offices, to the consternation of officials. The movement has grown, however, to encompass a much greater ideal. It offers endless possibilities of expression, less destructive than graffiti tags but no less effective. Graffiti doesn't have to involve the defacement of property; vegetable-style graffiti may take a bit more patience and planning than tagging, but in return it offers much satisfaction and the tra-la-la joy of sharing beauty with passersby. An easy and gratifying means of altering your landscape is through seeds. If you live in an apartment and have the luxury of a short wait for the bus, take a glance at your surroundings. Like most bus stops in cities, it is undoubtedly adjacent to an apartment building or office complex, with a boring rhododendron ghetto and lots of

---

Reclaim The Streets contribution to MayDay in London is a m

Armed with trowels, seeds, and imagination, the idea is to garden everywhere and anywhere. An urban adventure at the threshold of nature and culture, Guerrilla Gardening is about taking back our own time and space from capital.
Guerrilla Gardening is creative autonomous work, work that is about LIVING, not "working" to "make a living".

Picture thousands of Guerrilla Gardeners, they have come to take back what was once theirs, to transform a symbol of capitalism, to return urban land to its real usefulness - as provider of food, as public space where people meet face to face, discuss and

PARTICIPATE DIRECTLY IN THE REMAKING OF THEIR OWN CITY.

Guerrilla Gardening is _not_ a street party. It is an action demandir everyones participation and preparation. An adventure beyond specta

COME PREPARED! START SOWING THE SEEDS

Come prepared, and ready to get your hands dirty. Bring with you everything you need to make a Guerrilla Garden: saplings and seed earth and containers-subvert the packaging of capital: turn desig trainers into plant pots, traffic cones into hanging baskets. A b of earth, and a bottle of water to water your plants.
Vegetable seedlings, flowers, herbs, fertile green fingers and re hot desires, and all you need for merrymaking. Start planting now

Resistance is fertil

bare bark-o-mulch in between. It's an ideal spot to start altering the landscape; think of it as blank canvas.

Soil: Where life starts.

If you can't find any, make your own by composting, using organic waste, weeds or horse manure from riding schools or your local police station. The art of composting is looked at in the Urban Gardening section.

Often you can still find soil beneath tarmac and paving stones. Look out for building sites, where top soil has been piled up for landscaping.

If there is really not much soil about or you want to grow tomatoes on concrete, try the splendid Hugel bed technique.

Gather materials such as branches and wood for the bottom. This creates a breeding ground for beneficial insects who will speed up decomposition. Then layer on twigs, brambles and sticks to create volume and anchor all the thinner material. Next go layers of green and brown material: leaves, paper, cardboard, manure and straw for the brown, grass clippings, weeds, nettles, and anything similar for the green. Finally, cover the top with soil or finished compost to plant into. If there is not much available just use a handful where you have planted seeds or seedlings.

Get the bed at least one foot off the concrete— it will settle as it decomposes, providing nutrients for your garden for decades. That's it. This can be used just about anywhere, especially carparks. In gardens, mulch the bottom of the Hugel bed with cardboard or carpet to stop weeds coming through.

the splendid Hugel Bed technique

drawing by Greg Jalbert

brush, alternating layers of dry leaves, green material and manure, topped with a layer of finished compost or soil. note roots starting to bust through concrete.

If you have the chance, find out about the soil's history. If it's likely to be contaminated, for example if there's a nearby garage, then use non-edible plants or fruit trees, or build a Hugel bed on top of it.

Use weeds to tell you what state the soil's in and plant green manures if you are not likely to use it straight away (although you can combine green manures with planting). Armed with trowels, seeds, and vision, the idea is to garden everywhere. Anywhere.

What to plant?

Vegetables!

Start in pots in early spring, or direct seed on the day of! Unless you are coming back to water your guerrilla

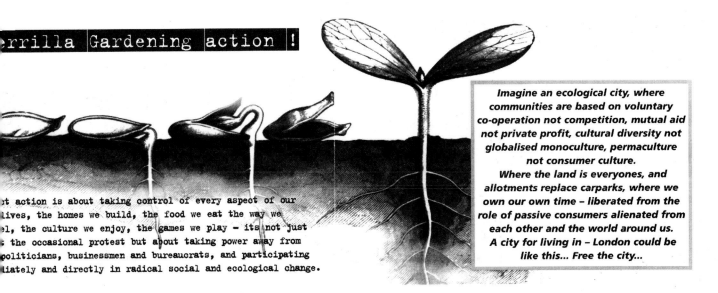

rrilla Gardening action !

t action is about taking control of every aspect of our lives, the homes we build, the food we eat the way we l, the culture we enjoy, the games we play — its not just the occasional protest but about taking power away from politicians, businessmen and bureaucrats, and participating iately and directly in radical social and ecological change.

Imagine an ecological city, where communities are based on voluntary co-operation not competition, mutual aid not private profit, cultural diversity not globalised monoculture, permaculture not consumer culture.
Where the land is everyones, and allotments replace carparks, where we own our own time – liberated from the role of passive consumers alienated from each other and the world around us.
A city for living in – London could be like this... Free the city...

garden, choose plants that can survive on local rainfall—remember that vegetable seedlings need regular moisture while they're young. Or plant in a city park or median strip that gets watered by city sprinklers!

Flowers!

The best option is to get some that are already potted, or try fast-growing, hardy seeds that can be neglected. The best time to sow these is in autumn or very early spring. Hardy annuals produce seeds the first year. Biennials are plants that live for two years. The first year they put up leaves, the second, they bloom, set seed, and die. Biennial seeds are best sown in autumn.

Much like canons or a round in a song, the trick to these plants is to start them in succession. Once they are established they will reseed and continue for years. Perennials are plants that can live for several years or more. Some easy perennials to grow from seed are evening primrose, lupines and oriental poppies. Check local gardening guides for flowers likely to thrive in your area.

Trees! Bushes!

A tactic proposed by guerrilla gardeners in Washington, D.C. is to take trees door-to-door in your neighborhood, offering to plant them for anyone who agrees to water and care for them. In one neighborhood kids pick peaches from the trees around their apartment and sell them to neighbors.

If you don't have city sprinklers to water your trees, you'll have to water them yourself. Two people can haul 30 gallons of water on a skateboard. Or you can divert street runoff to water your trees.

Grafting apple branches on crabapple trees or wild plums growing in alleys or over fences can have wonderful results. You can graft many branches onto each tree, each with its own variety of fruit.

Green Manures!

Green manures are plants grown to fertilize and create soil the lazy way. Rake the soil surface, removing big rocks and other non-organic material, spread seeds liberally, rake lightly again, water or wait for the rain. Fava or bell beans can be planted in the fall; clover, alfalfa and buckwheat can be planted in the early spring. The ground will slowly start living

again, and with a bit of luck plants will reseed and build up earth by themselves over time.

The cheap and easy way to do it is to buy mustard seeds, clover, alfalfa, buckwheat (the kind sold for sprouting), and fava beans from your local market. Comfrey can be found around. Dig out bits of roots and put them everywhere. It grows extremely fast, spreads and is excellent in compost.

Armed with trowels, seed and vision, the idea is to garden everywhere.

Where to plant?

As we've established, everywhere is the best option. There are a few things to take into account:

• Climate: does your plant like sun or shade? Fruit or tropical plants enjoy full exposure, as opposed to strawberries, wild garlic or lettuces and other greens who do better next to or beneath other plants.

• Space: is your plant a climber (beans grow around lamp-posts, peas on mesh fences). How big does your plant get compared to the space available? Is it likely to be spotted or trodden on?

• Soil is it? Herbs thrive on poor soils, root vegetables in sandy light soils, fast growing plants (eg. tomatoes or squash) in rich soil. Contaminated land can host flowers, non eatables, and fruit trees. The toxins will be contained within the wood, and the fruit won't be affected.

How to transport?

Bag up roots of trees to keep exposure to the air as low as possible. Place your flats in cardboard boxes and cut the bottom of plastic bottles to place on top of your pots (if you have to move the leaves around to fit them in, remember most plants prefer having their leaves turned upwards). Tape it all together for transportation.

For more information on the permaculture techniques discussed in this section, see Appendix, p100-117

Recipe for rhubarb crumble, just like ma used to make!

Just a little tip for all would be gardeners out there. Rhubarb is a particularly good plant for breaking up concrete. Just take rhubarb seed and stuff it in cracks in concrete. Then sit back and watch the crumble take shape!

Rhubarb can then be used to make crumbles and particularly fine wine, just the ticket for celebrating your newly green space.

Trees such as sycamore are also very resilient. They will quite happily spring up in small gaps and holes 'round the edges of buildings. This will then cause some serious structural damage, if allowed to take hold. Of ourse I'd never condone such things like trees and rhubarb. Have fun... I can't wait!

Guerrilla Gardens vs. the FBI

Washington D.C, April 16, 2001

an interview with an anonymous gardener

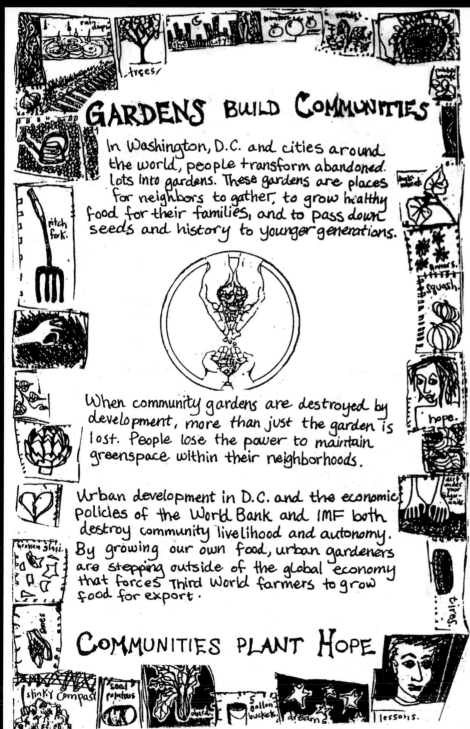

GARDENS BUILD COMMUNITIES

In Washington, D.C. and cities around the world, people transform abandoned lots into gardens. These gardens are places for neighbors to gather, to grow healthy food for their families, and to pass down seeds and history to younger generations.

When community gardens are destroyed by development, more than just the garden is lost. People lose the power to maintain greenspace within their neighborhoods.

Urban development in D.C. and the economic policies of the World Bank and IMF both destroy community livelihood and autonomy. By growing our own food, urban gardeners are stepping outside of the global economy that forces Third World farmers to grow food for export.

COMMUNITIES PLANT HOPE

flyer from a Guerrilla Gardening action, Washington, D.C., 4/15/00

flyer by Andrea, clea and Kevin, drawings by Abby Turtle

"We sat and blocked off a street for a little while, but then we got bored so we said, "Let's go do some gardening." It was the only thing that made sense. We went to the Women's Art Museum, and that inspired us, so then we went down to the FBI. We said, "Oh this is the FBI building— look at all those flower beds." It was full of pansies and shit. So we said, let's grow food! You could look over this five-foot-tall brick wall, and there was this cafeteria where the agents all went down to eat their lunches. It looked out on this courtyard, and there were two or three trees growing, but that was it for looking out at nature.

"So after we did all the flowerbeds we just sprinkled the rest of the seed down there. It was an area that didn't have any sliding doors so they weren't able to maintain it. That was probably why they only had trees there. So I said, "Something's gonna happen. Once that gets seeded with this wild chard and orach, it's gonna be there to stay. It's native to here, and it wants to come back."

Taking Trees out of the Private Sector

Oakland, CA

Tim Krupnik

It was 10 PM on a drizzly night in Oakland when the cop shouted, "Up against the wall! Drop that thing!" A three-foot spade with a green handle slipped from my shoulder to the concrete below. "I'll be damned, Scotty," explained the officer's partner. "That's not a shot gun, that's just a shovel!" My friend Dan, who was lugging around a bike cart full of fruit trees—apples, lemons, plums—burst out laughing. "Yeah, just a shovel. We're only planting trees!"

If your garden is lacking a vital element— fruit trees— it's time to think big. You needn't be constrained by a lack of garden space. There's plenty of arable land around, if you're willing to take it back. In America's cities, public parks and median strips on multi-lane roads are considered city or public property. And more often than not, you'll see handfuls of welfare-to-work people out there mowing away to keep these lawns well manicured. While grass is nice to sit on, it's not really that useful in cities where access to healthy, fresh food is a serious problem.

We've found that most city landscapers don't really mind if they suddenly come upon a persimmon tree that mysteriously popped up in the middle of the night. The better the trees presentation—staked, mulched, and roped off—the better chance it has to survive the city worker's hungry lawnmowers. Fruit trees can be strategically planted, either within reach of sprinkler systems in parks or irrigated median strips, or in hard-to-get-to places where the mowers are unlikely to shred them.

And it need not stop at parks. Technically, the sidewalks in front of homes and businesses are owned by the city, but must be maintained by the adjacent building owner. City councils in the States often plant "regular" trees— Sycamores, Oaks, etc—in these spots.

If you're worried about the soil, take a minute to look into the history of the park. Older people in the neighborhood will love to tell you about it, and it's a good chance to bond with people. If you found out that the area used to be a gas station, factory site dump, then it's probably a bad idea to plant there. Otherwise, trees are remarkably good at remedi-

young fruit trees in Oakland, CA

ating toxins in the soil while protecting their seeds, which are located in the fruit of the trees. Consequently, your apples, plums, cherries and avocados will be fine for a mid-afternoon snack. Nurseries will often give away trees that are "oddly shaped," root-bound, or that they are having trouble selling.

My friend Steve, a landscape architect once said, "While I was in school they always told me not to design in useful trees in public places—like in the sidewalk. Now I understand why. Free food means people will go to the grocery stores like Safeway less and less. They'll hang out in their neighborhoods more and more. And with that they'll feel more and more like a community. And I've realized that that's not necessarily what city planners want from the inner cities. Instead of empowered, they want to keep people subdued."

So do your part for community empowerment. Plant a fruit tree in a public place. In ten years when it's bearing lots of fruit, it will have become a hub of community life. With public fruit trees, we can shift from a lack of quality food in the inner cities to an abundance of fruit to pass on to our neighbors.

For more information fruit trees and street orchards, see Appendix, pages 104 and 109-111.

Swaling a Parking Lot
Dan Dorsey

As inhabitants of dryland climates know, one summer thundershower can turn urban streets into rivers. They see the abundance of water during these brief showers and the shortage of it during other times of the year, yet city planners in drylands still look on stormwater runoff as a problem.

Large cities such as Tucson bring Colorado River water from hundreds of miles away. Perhaps it's time that US drylanders join the rest of the world in seeing runoff as a precious resource, rather than something to be drained away as fast as possible. We need to publicize water-harvesting projects, the more the better.

The parking lot before asphalt was removed to make the swale. The curved white line follows the contour of the land and shows where the asphalt will be removed.

One example of a water harvesting project is a swaled parking area in Tucson. Working with Punch Woods, director of the Community Food Bank, I designed a system to harvest runoff which can be applied to any paved area. Janet Miller directed the installation of the project two years ago. First, using a bunyip water level and spray paint, we established contour lines throughout the parking lot and around the building. Then we brought in heavy equipment to precisely rip up the asphalt along the contour lines.

We ripped up strips of asphalt and removed some of the dirt underneath to form shallow concave swales and basins that would hold water. We planted hardy 15-gallon Chilean mesquites in the swales, put down barriers to prevent cars from running over the newly planted trees and repainted the parking lines to run along the new curvilinear swales. Altogether, we planted some 50 trees in the swales and in basins around the building.

After the first year, the trees required no watering, and due to all the water they receive, some mesquites are now 25 feet tall. This simple project has reduced the amount of water flooding the street during storms, reduced the energy bills for the building and created a pleasant place for clients and workers. If this project were repeated throughout the city, Tucson could end its flooding problems while creating a green, cool oasis.

I am always amazed to see real dirt under asphalt of concrete— we have gotten used to thinking of asphalt and concrete as a permanent covering, when, in fact, it is quite easy to rip it up to plant trees.

Update: The trees we planted continue to grow, even though the building has remained unrented for two years. To me, this is the mark of a truly sustainable project one that continues to thrive without additional input. Truly, all desert communities could be covered with trees using only available runoff from streets and buildings.

For information on constructing swales in parking lots and streets, see page 114. For information on other broadscale water harvesting and restoration techniques, see pages 70 and 114-115.

The swale planted with drought-tolerant native trees.

Gardening in the Concrete Jungle

New York, NY

John Plantain

Hey folks, this is John Plantain for gardening tips in your local concrete desert. Every day in America, 6000 acres of earth that could be used to grow food are paved over for more roads, parking lots and shopping malls. To reclaim our land we must first make topsoil as much of it has eroded into our storm drains, creeks and rivers to be washed out into the sea.

The easiest way to make some quick topsoil in the city is to dumpster a crate or garbage bag (a large amount because it will shrink) of old lettuce or other greens from your local supermarket. Make several layers in a wooden crate with a couple inches of washed out soil you might find in a construction site or park and let it sit in the sun and the rain for a few weeks (if there is no rain water your pile). The greens will turn into brown highly nitrogenous plant food and will be ready to stir up with the rest of the mix. Bravo, soil maker!

Break up concrete with a sledge or jack hammer and line up the resulting chunks along a planting bed to keep the soil from washing away.

If you have to retreat to a rooftop the battle is not over yet. Lay down a layer of plastic on your roof and mix your finished "greens" soil in a bucket with perlite or some other light-weight material. This is to keep the soil light so the roof doesn't collapse on your head as you contemplate the world's problems. Then put a beautiful layer of homemade soil on the top, and cover it with more greens or fallen leaves if available (this is to keep the moisture in and the soil critters alive).

Scared for your veggies in the harsh paved climate? Grow weeds! Here are some of the toughest plants alive and their uses.

Lamb's Quarters

Yielding 50,000 seeds a year this prolific weed is a close relative to spinach and has even more nutrient value (large amounts of vitamin A, C and calcium as well as many others). Its seeds have the ability to exist under concrete for twenty to thirty years

Winter Purslane (¼ natural size).

and still sprout up. Peasants and paupers used to use its seed as a grain when the wheat crops had been destroyed by the latest war.

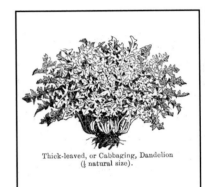
Thick-leaved, or Cabbaging, Dandelion (⅓ natural size).

Japanese Knotweed

This bamboo related shrub has a delicious lemon flavor when first sprouting up. It is an awesome pavement destroyer, I've seen its tasty sprouts pierce many a blacktop.

Mugwort

Often taking up whole sidewalks with its woody shoots this prolific, pleasant scented herb is the most common plant in New York City. Its calming fronds can be used in tea to put the sleepless to sleep and the dreamless to dream. It has also been known to prevent epileptic seizures. Its greenery is very good for making soil.

Plantain

Especially loving the CRACKS in pavement this plant is both edible and medicinal. The seeds are high in protein. Plantain leaves, well chewed, lessen the pain and swelling from bee stings and infected wounds and will help heal any cut or abrasion of the skin.

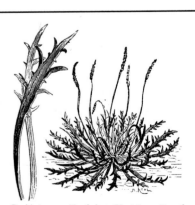
Buck's-horn or Hart's-horn Plantain, or Star of the Earth (½ natural size; separate leaves, ½ natural size).

Food for anarchists, the homeless, workers, philosophers

Ljubljana, Slovenia

Tomaz Petauer,
translated by Tea Hvala

When developers vy for profitable urban space, many of us are forced up rather than out. In apartments, the only work we do with the ground beneath our feet is bangin' the floor with the broom when our downstairs neighbor's music gets too loud. Without a garden plot, is it still possible to grow food? I remember my mom used to stuff ferns, grandma's christmas cactus and other houseplants in front of the window. We didn't think about growing vegetables—that was for people with the privilege of houses and yards. In Eastern Europe, many people have similar assumptions. "We can't garden in a city like Prague, not Athens, not Istanbul." If you think space is tight in New York, try an 8000-year-old city.

So I was overjoyed to to hear of a man in Ljubljana, Slovenia growing a significant portion of his vegetables 'way up off the ground in his flat. I met Tomaz over a beer and coffee and learned of his experiences with food and self sufficiency. What follows is an excerpt from his book. The information applies equally well to rooftops, porches, stairs, your bedroom, or wherever a planter box will fit. This direct, practical advice on growing food where there is no land is another step, another possibity in taking back our power. — S.E. Frass

If you don't have a garden that doesn't mean you have to give up on growing your own food: you can also do it on your balcony, terrace or indoors. Balconies are suitable for potatoes, tomatoes, peppers, pole beans, cucumbers and other vegetables. Tomatoes and cucumbers don't tolerate each other so you need to put them on opposite sides of the balcony. You should also remember that cucumbers need plenty of fertile soil and demand regular watering in summer heat. Pole beans are very convenient since they grow upwards, spirally clenching the bars of your balcony's railing. Above the railing, you can attach strings and make it possible for the plants to rise up to the ceiling of the balcony. Don't forget to provide support bars for tomatoes as well since they can grow so large that they will eventually overshadow all other vegetables.

As in organic gardening, you have to follow the rule of "good neigh-bors" (as mentioned, tomatoes and cucumbers are "bad neighbors") and plant tomatoes with carrots, onions (or

a balcony garden chock-full of food

garlic) and parsley; peppers with lettuce and radishes; beans with lettuce, radish and cucumbers (or tomatoes).

For successful gardening your balcony should be exposed to sunlight and have the kind of railing which lets the sunlight through (a concrete wall doesn't!). You can put plastic foil in between railing bars to protect your

Winter Purslane (⅓ natural size).

American, or Belle-Isle, Cress (⅓ natural size).

plants from the wind. Plants are not overly sensitive to cold, as least not as much as we tend to think. The real trouble-maker is wind because it dries the plants out and causes structural damage which— combined with cold— can kill the plants that could have resisted cold itself. If you have access to fiber folium (also known as Remay or row cover) you can cover the plants with it for extra protection. However, the most efficient solution is to install glass windows on your balcony. In this way you can turn it into a greenhouse that receives heat from your flat as well as from the sun.

It's easy to devote time to plants that grow on your balcony and elsewhere in the flat. Proportionally, the harvest is usually very rich. I used my own (still unripe) compost, and planted an area one meter square. I harvested 30 kilos of tomatoes, 8 kilos of peppers which I grew in boxes normally used for decorative flowers, or 6 kilos of potatoes. I fertilized the soil with pigeon manure that I collected from windowsills and from below other places where pigeons usually hang out.

Compost is stored best in wooden crates: when one is full you can put another crate on top of it. When the compost is finished, you remove it from the bottom. If you have followed the instructions and made sure that there is some air flowing through your compost, then you don't have to worry about the stench. Stale mineral water is rich in

microelements and you can use it for watering. Liquid fertilizer made from stinging nettles or other herbs also works out fine; both are economical, efficient and ecological.

Indoors, you can germinate wheat seeds, grow wheatgrass and use your windowsills to grow different plants in cases, boxes and pots. In winter, plants such as parsley, garden cress, chicory, chives and other

Chicory, or Succory (blanched), (⅓ natural size).

herbs work out perfectly well. Herbs grow well in light and sunny places, although some of them (celery, peppermint, balm mint, chives, water and garden cress, chervil, etc.) also grow in darker places. Homegrown herbs can be used fresh; dry them only when you can't use them all at once. Mild-tasting herbs can be used in larger quantities for salads or eaten by themselves, especially in winter when they partly cover our daily needs for vitamins. Besides, why shut ourselves away from the burning summer sun with curtains and shutters when we can use plants to do the same— and use the sunlight! Basil, for instance, certainly won't disappoint you.

why shut ourselves away from the burning summer sun with curtains and shutters when we can use plants to do the same—and use the sunlight!

Watercress can be grown in large jars with holes made especially for this purpose, and you can cut the plant as it grows through these holes. Nasturtiums taste very similar cress, and its seeds are much easier to collect, young leaves contain twice as much vitamin C as cress and five times as much as lemon does. Instead of chives you can plant green onions or garlic and use their growing bodies, which are rich in vitamins and minerals. For onions, garlic, cress, chives, parsley and chicory, you can cut the older leaves, leaving the newly grown leaves untouched.

edible nasturtium: tall (left, 1/25 natural size) and dwarf (right) 1/10 natural size

Beekeeping for the Intrepid

Oakland, CA

K. Ruby

For the last two years I have been a beekeeper. It puts me into yet another wingnut underground of the world. And perhaps I am even weirder than most, as I am relatively young, politically active and urban. A friend recently asked me, when I told her I'd been keeping bees, "I don't get it, what's the appeal?" As I tried to explain my fascination with the bees I reverted to telling about the bees themselves, the many roles they carry out in the hive during their short lifetime, the way they communicate through "bee dances," the amazing precision with which they do what they do.

Among the beekeeping group we tend about 5 or 6 colonies of bees or individual hives. These are in backyards in various parts of the East Bay and there is one in a local community garden. We have experience with two different hive box systems, the traditional Langstroth System, which are the square white boxes most Americans associate with beekeeping, and the Kenyan Top Bar System (KTBS) which was developed by the peace corps in Africa and is widely used there. There is ongoing discussion as to which system is "better." Each beekeeper insists that one or the other is healthier for the bees, but we have observed strong and weak colonies in both types of hives.

working a top-bar beehive in Oakland, CA

After experiencing both, most of us agree that we like the Kenyan system better for a number of reasons:

1. The KTBS can be built with cheap lumber and basic tools. The Langstroth System requires a higher initial cash input for the equipment and/or high quality lumber and really exact carpentry skills.

2. In the Langstroth sytem the combs are constructed by the bees in square frames. At harvest the tops of the combs are cut off and the honey is extracted in a centrifuge. Thus, more equipment and honestly, more work. In the top bar system the bees build "free form" from the top bar, filling out the comb to fit within the hive box. At harvest the comb is cut from the bar, mashed and extracted by gravity. We extract our honey using a white plastic bucket with holes drilled in the bottom and a screen. Again, a low investment process. It may be slightly worse for the bees, as they have to make new comb every time, but thus far, we haven't noticed the difference.

3. In working with the KTBS it is possible to close the hive as you work. Only two combs are open to the air at any one time and thus being overwhelmed with angry bees while working is minimized. In the traditional system when the top of the box is open, the entire hive has access to the air.

There are many reasons to become a beekeeper. It's fun. It's dangerous. You get to wear a funny costume and hang out with one of the most interesting creatures around. There is a special connection to nature, to plant cycles and to food próduction that you don't normally get to experience in our consumer culture. You support the magical process of pollination and support the setting of seed. It is a low cost backyard addition to an urban farm. The honey!!! Getting sticky stuff everywhere to the dismay of your housemates (mother, boy/girlfriend) and then making it up to them by feeding them honey in their tea and on their biscuits. Whichever system you choose, there are many reasons to become a beekeeper.

Check out the Resources section for more information on KTHB's, beekeeping and bees.

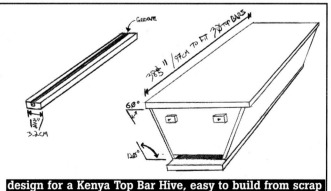

design for a Kenya Top Bar Hive, easy to build from scrap

Wild Pollinators

everywhere

by K. Ruby

Most people know that plants reproduce through pollination and setting seed. We are less aware that flowering plants depend on the services of an insect or animal pollinator to transport the male genetic material (pollen) to the female reproductive organs of another plant of the same species. There are many thousands of insect pollinators such as beetles, butterflies and moths and animal pollinators such as hummingbirds and bats, but bees (hymenoptera) are the most prolific and efficient of the pollinators. Their bodies are covered with fine hairs and physical structures designed specifically for pollen collection. There are over 25,000 species of bees worldwide and 4000 native species counted in the US.

Bees are generally divided into several categories. There are social and solitary bees, generalist and specialist bees. Honey bees are the only truly social bees. They live year round within a social structure, called a colony or hive, with a clear division of labor and they care for their young. The honey bee (*Apis mellifera*) is native to Europe, but has naturalized worldwide.

Bumble bees, some species of which are native to the US, are in the same genus as the honey bee and are considered semi-social. The queen bee builds a seasonal colony which works and lives together during the warm months of food abundance and dies out over the winter (mature bees overwinter in a dormant state waiting to hatch in the next warm season). Bumble bees are important pollinators and have a special relationship to certain plants who will only release their pollen through the strong vibrations of the honey bee's buzz. In particular bumble bees are pollinators for some plants of the Solanaceae family and are often used commercially as pollinators in tomato hothouses.

All the other bees are solitary bees. They may share nesting areas, but they build and live alone and do not tend their young once the egg is laid. Among these bees are the mason bees, carpenter bees, plasterer bees, digger bees and carpenter bees. They range widely in size and shape and in the manner of building their nests. Nests are commonly built in snags (dead wood) or directly in the ground and are lined with gathered material such as leaves or mud. The female bee hatches, mates and sets about building a nest. For each cell she collects pollen and mixes it with nectar to form a perfectly round pollen ball. This ball or "bee bread" as it is often called, is deposited into a cell and a single egg is laid on top of it. The bee then closes the cell and leaves. Nests can range from one to sixty cells, depnding on the species. Once the egg hatches, the larva eats, poops and pupates. Depending on the species and the time of year the mature bee will then emerge and start the cycle over, or over winter in a semi dormant state, waiting for the right weather conditions. They will often emerge just at the moment that their prefered host plant is coming into bloom!

Bees fly from flower to flower, gathering food (nectar and pollen) for themselves and their young. Along the way, the fine hairs on their bodies, charged with electrostatics, pick up pollen which is deposited when they stop at the next flower. Some bees are generalists—they gather from all different flowers. Others are specialists who have developed an evolutionary relationship with a particular plant. Their life cycle and anatomy may be attuned to this plant in such a way that if one is

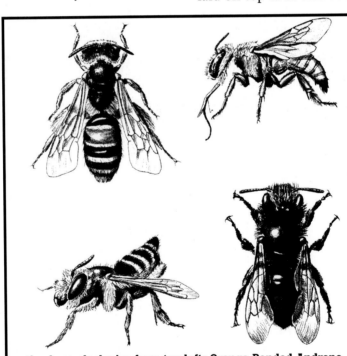

native bees clockwise from top left: Orange Banded Andrena, Resin bee, Short Leafcutter Bee, Metallic Leafcutter Bee

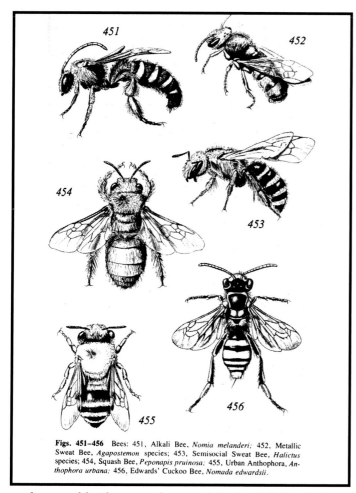

Figs. 451–456 Bees: 451, Alkali Bee, *Nomia melanderi;* 452, Metallic Sweat Bee, *Agapostemon* species; 453, Semisocial Sweat Bee, *Halictus* species; 454, Squash Bee, *Peponapis pruinosa;* 455, Urban Anthophora, *Anthophora urbana;* 456, Edwards' Cuckoo Bee, *Nomada edwardsii.*

milkweed, ceonothus, grindelia, fireweed, verbena and dusty miller. To provide and maintain a regular visiting spot 2 to 3 square meters of plant material seems to be a good minimum. If you provide water in a small pond or bird bath, be sure that there are plenty of landing areas for the bees. Flat rocks or sticks that angle gradually into the water are excellent for this purpose.

Native bees are a vital link in the cycle of life and their role in the continuance of these cycles is often underestimated. Every time a species becomes extinct we loose access to valuable information and wisdom contained in the gene sequence. Gene pool diversity is not only important to human applications, it is valuable in itself. Once that information is lost, we can no longer get it back; we can only wait and see how this loss may affect the complex and interconnected web of life. At this very moment we stand at the crux of mass species extinction. We have a choice to support life or destroy it. Creating habitat for bees and plants is a simple, fun and deeply satisfying. Happy Pollinating!

More information on native bee life cycles and creating native bee habitats can be found at: www.Xerxes.org/poll/home.htm

FYI. All female bees have the capacity to sting. No male bees can sting. Most bees, when left to themselves and unthreatened will not sting. If a bee approaches you, it is possible that you smell good to them, like a flower! If you walk away calmly and avoid making abrupt movements you are also unlikely to be stung.

endangered both are endangered. In the US this is happening all the time. Entire plant species have been destroyed through urban development and agricultural herbicides. Bee habitat is also disrupted through constant clearing of deadwood and tilling of soil where bees nest.

Fortunately, native bees can be quite enduring. Even specialist bees can learn to survive on other plants than their host plant. Bees will return to an area that has been decimated given the right conditions and can exist quite well even in an urban setting given enough of the right kind of habitat. In a recent study by UC Berkeley professors and botanists, 72 native bee species were counted in the Berkeley area alone.

Native bees need much the same things as we do; shelter. food, water and a place to raise their young. Bee habitat can be provided by creatively arranging stumps or other deadwood in your garden and by leaving exposed earth in perenial plant beds unturned. You can also create bee habitat by drilling holes into scrap lumber. Native bees prefer a range of diameters between 3/16" and 5/16" and between 4 and 8 inches deep.

Due to selective color vision bees like flowers in the white, yellow, blue and purple ranges. There are many many native and exotic plants that will draw bees to your yard. Among them are mints, lavenders, yarrow, clarkia, gaillardia, delphinium, poppies, penstamon,

Building for Bees

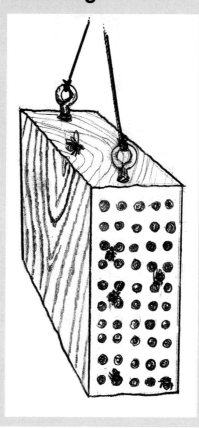

The pollinator services of the Blue Orchard Mason Bee, known to farmers and entomologists as 'BOB,' are increasingly used in commercial orchards as they are more resistant to mites and American foulbrood which have decimated honey bee populations in the US in the last 10 years. A piece of scrap lumber with 3/16"-5/16" holes drilled in one or both ends provides a place for Blue Orchard Mason bees to lay their eggs; mount on a post or hang from a tree.

Guerrilla Solar

The unauthorized placement of renewable energy on a utility grid

Lauraxe

Energy is freely and democratically provided by nature. This century's monopolization of energy by utilities both public and private threatens the health of our environment. Solar guerrillas believe that clean renewable energy should be welcomed by utilities. But utilities and governments continue to put up unreasonable barriers to interconnection, pushing common citizens to solar disobedience.

Guerrilla systems share clean, renewable energy with the utility grid and reduce the need for polluting generation plants. They do not endanger utility line workers, as utility companies contend. When interconnection for small-scale renewables becomes fair, simple, and easily accessible to all, there will be no more need for guerrilla action.

PROFILE: 0014

DATE: January, 2001

LOCATION: Somewhere in the USA

INSTALLER NAME: Classified

OWNER NAME: Classified

INTERTIED UTILITY: Classified

SYSTEM SIZE: 120 Watts of PV

TIME IN SERVICE: 2 years

Closer to the Inspector's headquarters than most, this guerrilla solar system is located in the heart of one of the largest metropolitan areas in the US. It consists of two 60 watt Solarex panels, wired in series to a 100-watt Trace Microsine intertie inverter, converting the DC electricity to AC. The inverter is skillfully wired to a handy extension cord, which is plugged into the wall outlet. Voila! A grid-intertie system, simple and easy to install. Notice the homemade frames on the panels, which had a short past life in an R&D lab as test panels. Now they live happily on the roof of our shed, sending their electrons to the utility grid.

This small solar-electric system is symbolic in relation to the total electrical energy use it offsets, but it is a concrete step we've taken to living sustainably in the city.

This small solar-electric system is symbolic in relation to the total electrical energy use it offsets, but it is a concrete step we've taken to living sustainably in the

city. As renters, it's hard to do big house alterations to change the way we live and decrease dependence on the environmentally destructive and wasteful infrastructures set up for us. But it's not impossible.

We can greatly reduce the electricity we consume. Solar panels can be installed on shed roofs (out of sight of conservative landlords), or attached like planter boxes outside the window of your house or apartment.

We're guerrilla energy producers, and also guerrilla energy savers. Our house is fully equipped with a graywater system. We re-use our shower water in the garden. This saves water stolen from dammed up river ecosystems, fosters water consciousness, and removes the "waste" water from city wastewater treatment plants, which consume vast quantities of electricity and dose the water with chemicals before discharging it. By saving water and returning it to nature's cycles, we're taking another step away from the environmentally destructive infrastructure so much of our lives are tied to.

Love,

The Revolutionary Photovoltaic Front
(Frente Revolucionario Fotovoltaico)

A Note on Guerrilla Solar

Some people are uncomfortable with war-terminology applied to positive environmental actions. In the case of guerrilla solar, we use the term "guerrilla" deliberately: a war is being waged upon the earth and all living inhabitants and we are fighting back. With guerrilla solar, guerrilla gardening and guerrilla greywater systems we are fighting against the destructive and oppressive infrastructure of modern society with the power of life.

three members of the Frente Revolucionario Photovoltaico next to their illegal, but highly functional rooftop grid-intertie photovoltaic system.

release massive amounts of energy, heating water to create steam, powering a turbine which spins electrons to the power grid connecting to our homes. Uranium mining has contaminated large areas of Native lands and scarce desert water sources. The "disposal" of nuclear waste causes cancer and birth defects in Native and low-income communities, and devastates the natural world.

Why, with our advanced technology, does it seem practically impossible to live sustainably? It's not. But until we live without electricity or produce our own power from solar, wind, or micro-hydro we are complicit in the destruction caused by power generation. Just as growing food in the city can decrease our dependence on the destructive industrial agriculture system, producing our own energy where we live allows us to disengage from the havoc wreaked by the power grid.

Guerrilla solar is one step towards taking responsibility for the true impacts of our modern lifestyles. By incorporating it into our daily existence, we fight the oppressive and destructive status quo as we create alternative ways to live.

The Guerrilla Solar profile first appeared in Home Power Magazine, the leading renewable energy magazine in the

Many people are concerned about toxic waste, global warming and deforestation but don't connect these problems with our lifestyles. The ripple effects of what we consume in our daily lives travel across oceans, over borders and beyond mountains. When we look a little closer we realize that we hold the power to stop this destruction.

The ripple effects of what we consume in our daily lives travel across oceans, over borders and beyond mountains. When we look a little closer we realize that we hold the power to stop this destruction.

Let's use coal, hydroelectric and nuclear power plants as examples:

Coal: companies rip into the hearts of mountains, often on Native lands, collecting and burning the black carbon rocks to make steam to spin turbines, generating electricity. The impacts of burning coal include respiratory illness in those who live near the plants, acid rain and global warming.

Hydro-electric: immense concrete structures rise hundreds of feet above the riverbed and stop water in its tracks. Forced down the penstock, water's weight and gravity slam into a turbine wheel, which spins and throws electrons into the powerlines. "Clean, renewable" hydroelectric power has impacted thousands of river ecosystems. Fish unable to swim to their spawning grounds above the dams go extinct, while cultures that rely on the fish and the river are decimated.

Nuclear power: atoms are split to

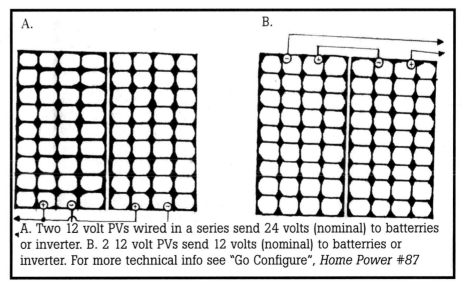

A. Two 12 volt PVs wired in a series send 24 volts (nominal) to batteries or inverter. B. 2 12 volt PVs send 12 volts (nominal) to batteries or inverter. For more technical info see "Go Configure", *Home Power #87*

Water & Graywater

Water is the universal solvent, seeping through hundreds of feet of soil and bedrock to underground aquifers, dissolving salts and fossils and everything else in its path. It cycles through rivers and oceans, ice caps, cumulus clouds, plants and animals, and is constantly transformed by these journeys. The water in your blood carries the memory of being part of fish, of some kid in China ans really old sycamore tree. The oceans of the future will become heavy with the salts the waters leach from the land. Glaciers will retreat and advance and retreat again. Water's physical structure and its constant transformation will remain.

Where does your water come from? If you live in a rainy place, you may not think it matters, though your water is no doubt polluted. Where does your food come from? If you buy any of it at the store the water to grow it comes from the Oglalla aquifer under the midwestern states, the Rio Colorado which irrigates the Southwest, and a handful of rivers in Northern California which supply water to the Central Valley. This water gets pumped uphill to the fields, mixes with petroleum-derived fertilizers, pesticides, and herbicides and runs off into rivers and streams. Industrially grown food is fossil fuels and water transmuted by technology. Shipped hundreds of miles (using more oil) to sterile supermarkets, the abundant harvests lull you into paying rock-bottom prices for it, without thinking of the true costs.

Our food supply depends on mined fossil fuel and groundwater, and industrial agriculture both mines and pollutes the soil. Even before the oil and water run out, much of the world's arable land will be permanently poisoned with salt. As deserts grow and rainfall patterns shift, some surface water will remain. We don't really need electricity, though we're addicted to the conveniences it brings. But when all our fertile soil is salted or washed into the ocean we, like the Sumerians and Hohokam of old, will realize that we never did live amidst limitless abundance.

Breaking the Water Cycle

In the global water cycle, water evaporates from the oceans. Clouds form over forests and mountains and rain falls. Above deserts it falls sporadically. Some rainwater infiltrates into the soil, percolating back into the water table. Some runs down rivers to the ocean, some evaporates and some drains into salt-pans.

We humans have tried to create our own water cycle. The East Bay's water travels from high in the Sierras, down the Mokelumne River, past a series of dams, through miles of aqueduct, concrete tunnels and steel pipes. It crosses the Coast Ranges through siphons and pumping stations, then is treated by chloramine and other toxic chemicals before flowing out the faucet. Most urban water follows a similar path.

1924, Yuba River, Sierra Nevada Mountains, CA: So many spawing salmon piled themselves against the base of the new Bullards Bar Dam that Pacific Gas & Electric workers torched them with gas to alleviate the stench

Unlike the natural water cycle, this system of aqueducts and reservoirs benefits only human enterprise: river life dies out, wetlands are drained, canyons and valleys disappear behind dams. Even the oceans are slowly dying.

Meanwhile, millions of gallons of rainwater fall onto city roofs and streets and run off into the sewers. If we catch this water and use it in our homes and gardens, we step outside of the destructive cycle of dammed rivers and depleted aquifers. Infiltrating the runoff from hillsides, roads and parking lots allows trees to grow. Under trees, natural systems regenerate through the cracks in the concrete. In the same way that composting creates rich soil from trash, water catchment and graywater cycling create opportunities for growth in barren places.

Cheap Salvage Water Catchment

Put a trash can under a downspout and you've got water for your garden. 55-gallon drums, available free from bakeries, can be linked together with PVC pipe to provide hundreds of gallons of water storage (Diagram 1, p. 94). Ferrocement tanks are also cheap to build, though they can crack in earthquake country. They can range in size from several to hundreds of gallons (Diagram 2). You can make a 1200 gallon cistern for under $20 using remesh, plastic and carpet (Digram 3). In dusty or polluted areas, you may want to build a system to discard the first water that falls on your roof, then diverts the clean water to your cistern (Diagram 4).

If your neighbor's roof drains near your garden, harvest their water too. Maybe they'll realize what a resource they're wasting.

When creating water catchment systems, let gravity move the water. If your yard slopes site the tank at the top of the slope. In flat areas elevate the tank a few feet off the ground on a pad of compacted dirt lined with rock or broken concrete.

Water tanks have a lot of thermal mass. They trap the sun's heat during the day and radiate it at night, so they can help protect sensitive plants like citrus and tomatoes from frost.

A tank elevated a few feet off the ground will not give you the same water pressure as the city reservoir.

Instead of sprinklers and gushing hoses, try using unglazed pots for irrigation. See page 105 (Pots also work great for irrigating from an elevated constructed wetland!)

Graywater

Even if you can't catch all your water from the sky, you can still reduce your dependence on dams and sewage treatment plants by using city water twice: once to bathe and wash clothes and dishes, and again in your garden. Water from showers, sinks and washing machines is called greywater. Far from being a waste product, it's safe to use for irrigation, and the soap that gives it its gray color contains phosphates and nitrates, nutrients that plants need to grow. Using graywater in your garden is easy and inexpensive if you live in a house. Aside from the obvious benefits of saving water (and money on your water bill), reusing graywater keeps it from polluting your local bodies of water via the sewer system and reconnects you and your garden to the natural water cycle.

Graywater treatment wetlands

In the natural world there are no sewage treatment plants to clean water. Marshes, bogs, swamps, wet meadows, tidal and riparian (streamside) wetlands are nature's own water purification systems. Wetlands are complex webs of water, substrate, plants, decomposing plant material, vertebrate and invertebrate animals and microorganisms. In this rich environment, physical, chemical and biological processes conspire to filter and precipitate silt and organic matter, transform excess nutrients into algae and plants and remove pollutants. Wetlands function like giant sponges, soaking up floodwaters and trapping sediment and nutrients that floods carry. They are crucial to the health of rivers and oceans, and provide habitat for an incredible diversity of bird an aquatic life. In the US, more than half of wetlands have been drained or filled in for development and agriculture; in the San Francisco Bay Area 95% of wetlands have been destroyed in the last hundred and fifty years.

Because of wetlands' ability to remove nutrients, chemical pollutants and heavy metals from the water, people

Sin Agua no hay Vida. Sin Tierra no hay Paz.
"Without water there is no life. Without land there can be no peace"
—a sticker found in Tucson, AZ

Millions of gallons of rainwater fall onto city roofs and streets and run off into the sewers. If we catch this water and use it in our homes and gardens, we step outside of the destructive cycle of dammed rivers and depleted aquifers.

Water Storage Solutions

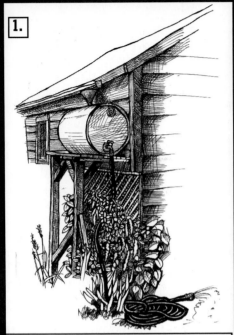

1.

harvesting water off a rooftop starts with a 55-gallon drum salvaged from a bakery and elevated to drain by gravity to the garden. barrels can be linked together to provide more water storage capacity.

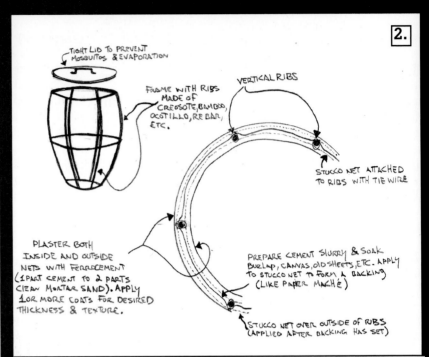

2.

TIGHT LID TO PREVENT MOSQUITOS & EVAPORATION

FRAME WITH RIBS MADE OF CREOSOTE, BAMBOO, OCOTILLO, REBAR, ETC.

VERTICAL RIBS

STUCCO NET ATTACHED TO RIBS WITH TIE WIRE

PLASTER BOTH INSIDE AND OUTSIDE NETS WITH FERROCEMENT (1 PART CEMENT TO 2 PARTS CLEAN MORTAR SAND). APPLY 1 OR MORE COATS FOR DESIRED THICKNESS & TEXTURE.

PREPARE CEMENT SLURRY & SOAK BURLAP, CANVAS, OLD SHEETS, ETC. APPLY TO STUCCO NET TO FORM A BACKING (LIKE PAPER MÂCHÉ)

STUCCO NET OVER OUTSIDE OF RIBS (APPLIED AFTER BACKING HAS SET)

A ferrocement water jar can hold from a few to a few hundred gallons of water, and is easily made from cement and recycled materials

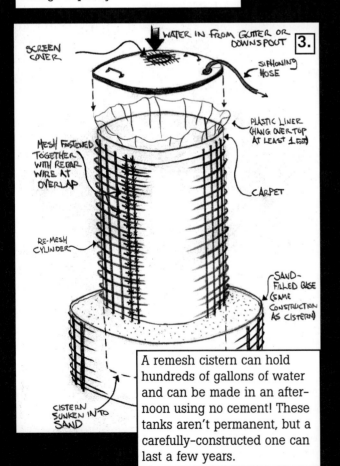

3.

SCREEN COVER

WATER IN FROM GUTTER OR DOWNSPOUT

SIPHONING HOSE

PLASTIC LINER (HANG OVER TOP AT LEAST 1 FOOT)

MESH FASTENED TOGETHER WITH REBAR WIRE AT OVERLAP

CARPET

RE-MESH CYLINDER

SAND-FILLED BASE (SAME CONSTRUCTION AS CISTERN)

CISTERN SUNKEN INTO SAND

A remesh cistern can hold hundreds of gallons of water and can be made in an afternoon using no cement! These tanks aren't permanent, but a carefully-constructed one can last a few years.

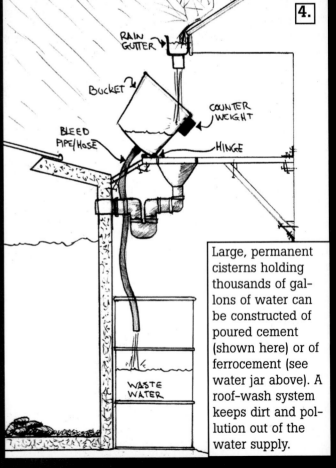

4.

RAIN GUTTER

BUCKET

COUNTER WEIGHT

BLEED PIPE/HOSE

HINGE

WASTE WATER

Large, permanent cisterns holding thousands of gallons of water can be constructed of poured cement (shown here) or of ferrocement (see water jar above). A roof-wash system keeps dirt and pollution out of the water supply.

have begun using them as an alternative to septic tanks and sewage treatment plants. They realize that by imitating natural systems, constructed wetlands transform polluting, energy intensive sewage treatment into beautiful ecosystems that produce methane gas for cooking or small-scale heat and power generation, plant material for compost and clean water for use in agriculture or landscaping. In Arcata, CA the municipal constructed wetlands is a beautiful place, filled with birds and wildlife, where kids learn about the natural world.

Constructed wetlands have important applications in rural situations as well. For example, a remote hospital in an autonomous Zapatista community in Chiapas purifies the hospital's wastewater in an area where the high water table makes a septic tank and leachfield a source of potential contamination to the nearby river and downstream communities.

However, in cities, drylands and other places where there is a critical scarcity of water, it doesn't make sense to use clean water just to dispose of excrement. In these situations, and in many rural situations as well, a better alternative is to compost human waste and use it in agriculture or for methane generation. (See Resources for information on composting humanure.)

Constructed wetlands can also be used to treat graywater. If you live

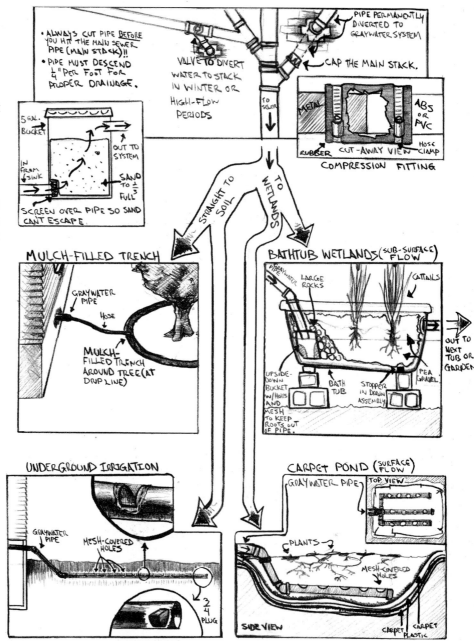

Four plans for graywater irrigation systems plus an optional sand filter. Systems can be constructed with scrap materials. See Resource section for details

in an apartment or grow mostly fruit trees or ornamental trees, you can use untreated graywater for all your irrigation needs. However, if you grow lots of veggies, you should treat your graywater with a constructed wetlands in an old bathtub before using it in your garden. As Laura Allen, co-founder of the Guerrilla Graywater Girls says, "Bringing the water purification process into your house by having a small wetland ecosystem in your backyard is a beautiful sight!"

Constructing a Wetland

Since 1999, the Guerrilla Graywater Girls have designed and built six constructed wetlands in Oakland, Seattle and Detroit, as well as several graywater systems without wetlands. All of them were built from mainly salvaged materials, using water from one or more bathrooms. The basin we use most often is a cheap steel

bathtub (cast iron is more expensive and way too heavy). Bathtubs come from salvage yards, dumps or renovation projects where they're tearing the old tub out. We've also salvaged (free or cheap) ABS and PVC pipe, fittings, 30 and 55 gallon barrels which act as surge tanks, utility sinks for smaller wetlands, plastic trash cans, lumber and scrap metal (to build structures which elevate the system so water can flow by gravity), hardware, garden hose, pond liner. Gravel comes from highway improvement projects, railroad tracks, or occasionally a soil products supplier. We dig up a few cattails from ditches along roadsides or other areas where they are abundant— we don't want to damage a fragile natural wetland to create a new one.

See Appendix, pages 105 & 108 for more ideas on using graywater in your garden. See the Resources section for more graywater and constructed wetlands information.

the Urban Wilds Project

cleo

Four kids from the after-school program where I work show up for the bike trip to Dimond Canyon in Oakland one afternoon in late November. We leave from the after-school center and ride down a busy avenue, weaving into traffic to dodge opening car doors. I have to shout to be heard above the cacophony of engines, screeching tires, bumpin' stereos, sirens, and the freeway's everpresent static roar. As we ride into the wide, grassy park, children's voices add to the mix. Sausal Creek (unheard) flows in a deep channel up against the backs of houses, the banks are reinforced with many layers of crumbling concrete. Even so, the eroding slopes continue to undercut fences and foundations.

We follow the creek upstream through the city park and cross a road. With each turn of the bike wheels, the rising walls of the steep canyon shut out more of the city's hum. Huge bay trees arch high overhead. The sound of water rushes into my eardrums. The richness of the sound and the growing silence that surrounds it push the city sounds out of my head. I haven't left the city for weeks; the green is dizzying.

The Works Progress Administration

In the 1930's the Works Progress Administration attempted to force the creek into a straight concrete channel. Without meanders, fallen logs and copses of willow to slow the floodwaters down and trap erosive silt, the destructive force of Sausal Creek at high water increased. The creekbed dropped deeper. In an attempt to stop the downcutting, the WPA built low concrete dams between the concrete walls. But the drop over the dam only magnified the water's force— below each dam is a large pothole where the churning water has undercut even the thick concrete walls.

Nonetheless, Dimond Canyon, minutes from the dense Fruitvale neighborhood where the after-school program is located, is one of the wildest spots in metropolitan Oakland. We bike along the creek into the gathering dusk. The low hum of the freeway seems hundreds of miles away. We get off our bikes under a concrete bridge spanning the canyon far above and look at the bright graffiti written on the gray walls far above. Suddenly, thirteen-year-old Ed says, "It's too quiet here. I can't take it. I want to go back to the city."

Urban Wilds

As cities grow, they displace the wild world. This city has crowded out the creeks with industrial parks, destroyed wetlands by filling them for airports and shoreline development, and sent wealthy suburbs crawling up into the steep, fire-prone slopes of the nearby hills. One has to travel several hours to feel the earth breathe and hear water flowing aboveground. Every day the wilds are farther from the city as thousands of acres of farm and wild land are turned into roads, subdivisions and stripmalls.

But what if we could restore the wilderness in the heart of the city? While development continues in ever-expanding circles, we could begin to create complex native ecosystems between office buildings, under overpasses, and in the sterile parks that dot the urban landscape. There is vacant land in even the densest neighborhoods, there is soil beneath the pavement: plants grow.

Urban Promise Academy students in their outdoor classroom

Beginning an urban wilds project can be as simple as throwing handfuls of native seeds in the back corner of your yard or vacant lot. Planting under a native tree or shrub (known as a nurse plant) will greatly increase their chance of survival. As the plants establish themselves, you'll notice an incredible increase in insects. Soon the air will hum with buggy noises and birdsong. If you make a small pond or wetland, you may find frogs or salamanders. As birds perch on a bush next to your pond, they'll plant the seed of the fruit they ate for breakfast. Over the years the diversity of plants and animals increases exponentially.

Presently the focus of most public urban wilds projects is on creek or wetlands restoration and so-called "invasive plant removal" (see sidebar). In Oakland, the Friends of Sausal Creek have been removing invasive ivy and scotch broom from the steep walls of Dimond Canyon for many years. They restored an area of riparian (creek-side) plants, as well as a section of native grasses and wildflowers. Over the years, they build up enough credibility with the city government that when the DPW needed to dig up an old leaking sewer pipe that runs under the creek, the Friends convinced them to replace the concrete channel with a meandering bed. Volunteers collected seed and cuttings from native plants growing higher in the watershed. With the help of dozens of school classes, they propagated more than 15,000 trees, bushes, grasses, wildflowers and riparian plants, then planted them along the new creekbed.

Tearing up streets for creeks

The techniques of creek and land restoration are based on traditional knowledge and common sense. The techniques used in revegetating bare soil and raising eroded creekbeds are not hard to learn. In a densely-populated urban setting, however, one cannot fence off an eroded dirtbike hill, much less jackhammer up a street to expose a creek, without having the support of the neighborhood. It will take a mass movement to restore urban watersheds from the hills to the bay. We started with middle-school students.

Grey Kolevzon and I hoped to build on the work that

Plants, people and biodiversity

David Graves, deep ecologist and environmental educator, wrote this letter in response to an article on the restoration of Sausal Creek. The proposed restoration project includes removing many of the WPA dams, re-digging the creek's channel to include more meanders, constructing brush and rock erosion-control structures, and planting willow copses to help control floods. The Friends of Sausal Creek, a local environmental organization that leads restoration workshops (focused strongly on "non-native" plant removal) for local youth. In line with this focus, they are proposing the removal of many plants from the sides of the canyons, including eucalyptus, poplar, and even some large native bay trees. Their goal is to provide enough sun for the willow plantings to thrive; in this letter to the editor, David points out some of the issues associated with their position.

Having had some years' experience in creek restoration here in San Francisco, I found the Sausal Creek account very interesting, since it brought to mind issues concerning plants, people and biodiversity found here as well.

Once a restorationist, I now consider myself a conservationist, in the sense that a restorationist, in my opinion, hopes to re-create an ecological condition of the past by his/her restoration of so-called native plants. A conservationist, on the other hand, looks at the broader picture of how evolution (including the human part in introducing so-called non-native plants) has come to a point where many animals have taken the opportunity to adapt to a broad array of plant life once not found here. And when I say adapt, I include the human animal, whose aesthetic appreciation for large trees must be acknowledged and respected.

And what about the Others (why must we always place the Others in a "non-human" category, as if they were negated by humans)? Many species of butterflies, for example, have adapted to so-called non-native plants and there exists no firm scientific basis, as far as I can determine, that these butterflies will adapt back to plants once widely established in a terrain far more pristine than our present industrially-degraded landscape. Degraded terrain, similar to a raked garden, is fertile ground for "non-natives" (oh, there's that term again!).

I often wonder, when I read of dedicated restorationists taking students armed to the teeth with weed wrenches into restoration areas to eradicate weeds, how these young people respond to the usual pep talks of "natives vs. non-natives." Many of these children come from immigrant families. I work with many similar young, impressionable minds in San Francisco, where the same question arises. Since they are not native to the United States, do these young people associate themselves with somehow being bad themselves?

These are a few reasons why I find the restorationist movement at best questionable scientifically, at worst damning educationally, in the sense that the teachable values of peaceful co-existence and multicultural tolerance are excluded from the restorationist philosophy.

Oh, by the way, I once questioned a native Californian about his own indigenous roots, seeking firm ground for where the term "native" came from. With a sly grin reminiscent of a wiley coyote, he answered: "Oh, we just pushed our way into the land, replacing whoever was there before us."

So much for the sanctity of what's native or not.

groups like the Friends of Sausal Creek were doing, and to give local kids more sense of ownership over the massive changes that had occurred in Dimond Park in the past year. We designed a watershed education curriculum for 6th graders which takes them on a journey through time and space to learn about their urban watershed.

observing native plants

Up in the hills, the redwood forest became our classroom, where the kids learned how redwood trees breathe water vapor up into the air which becomes clouds, and how fog condenses on redwood needles and drips down to the forest floor. They saw where Sausal creek first comes out of the ground, then followed it down through the city to where it emerges in San Leandro Bay.

testing the headwaters of Sausal Creek

Through their explorations they learned about plant communities, erosion and the impact of human settlement on the creek and its living inhabitants. They learned a little about scientific methodology by comparing the quality of the water, the width, depth and flow of the creek and the creatures living in the creek high in the watershed and down in the city. On the final canoe trip to a wetland in the bay, they looked up to the redwood forest where their journey began, and really understood

a lesson on the water cycle in the redwood forest

that they lived in a watershed, inside a larger natural ecosystem. And while most of their watershed was barely visible under the concrete, they came up with ideas—from picking up trash to recycling motor oil to gardening without pesticides to planting native plants— that could help their watershed live again.

Even more important than the science and the history they learned was the experience of becoming comfortable being outside in the woods. They explored the redwood forest silently for 5 minutes (a very difficult thing for an eleven year old) and felt the cool, still quiet of that ancient place wrap around them. They dug their fingers into the black soil under the trees and smelled the rich, clean earth. They felt the heat and the crunch of dry leaves underfoot in the chaparral-covered hillside, saw snakes and birds and lizards, and imagined they saw a few mountain lions. They got their feet wet in the creek, reached into the mud looking for insect larva, and grabbed onto the roots of a huge willow tree to climb down the washed-out banks below a culvert. These experiences changed the creek from a place to throw trash or cut class to a wild and exciting place worth saving.

Water underground

But what about the real creek that flows in a culvert underneath the park, the street and the school? If we could free the underground creek from its concrete tunnels, maybe the few steelhead and salmon who survive in a few areas would return and multiply. In order to do this, some people

fifth graders exploring the creek

might need to move, some roads might need to go, and some more jobs might need to be created in the area of urban watershed restoration. These changes seem inconceivable in this year 2002, yet we do all these things to build new roads and freeways, which ostensibly serve people, yet destroy land and pollute the air and water. By considering the living ecosystems within the cities which we have constructed with humans and our machines in mind, could we begin to figure out new ways to live in the city and the world?

These questions I leave for you to answer in your late-night rambles through the damp subsurface culverts, your steep scrambles down redwood canyons, your door-to-door wetlands plants giveaways and the rhythm of your boots on an uneven boulder trail. What I can say, from where I stand in the struggle, is that through the process of restoring degraded land I have tapped into deep springs of hope—a sense of wonder at the capacity of living systems to regenerate. Restoration work comes down to spreading mulch, piling up sticks, and an eye for throwing rocks around. At times, these simple actions seem futile against the backdrop of the continuing destruction of the natural world. Yet when the rains come, silt collects behind check dams, seed balls sprout and swales turn into green ribbons winding across the land. For all the thousands of acres that are paved and plowed and logged, this one spot is starting to live again.

My friend Joel once said that the best thing you can do to restore a watershed is walk from ridge to stream lining up sticks on contour. By this he meant several things.

First, that it's very important to walk the land you're working on again and again. Digging swales in the rain is particularly educational.

His second point was that if you make small changes in the landscape, notice the effects your actions have on the complex interactions of that particular place, you can avoid creating large problems you may not have anticipated. The WPA dams in Dimond Canyon are one small reason to work this way. These "flood-control" structures not only block spawning fish and destroy riparian ecosystems, they actually cause more severe flooding downstream.

Third, lining up sticks on contour takes no more energy than one would spend walking through the woods. A whole watershed covered with this type of microcatchment will have a much larger impact on flood control than a concrete dam in a fourth-order stream, because this type of structure keeps floodwaters from reaching the stream in the first place. Instead, they soak into the

soil and seep slowly down to the water table, nourishing plants and soil life on their way.

Perhaps most importantly, this way of working—patterned on the basic natural processes of the forest—reminds us that there's nothing new about the work we're doing. It's all been done before—and better—by the complex living systems to which we are intimately connected.

After Joel said his piece about lining up sticks, a student said "You permaculturists are always trying to control nature down to the finest detail. It's one thing to do it in your vegetable garden, but it's wrong to go messing with the forest like that." Joel replied that the point of permaculture is to figure out how to provide for your basic needs on as little land as possible so the rest of the land can be returned to the wild. They argued back and forth, each sure he was absolutely right.

I realized there was more to the story than either of them could see. So I spoke up. I said, "Look, in doing land restoration you try to create situations for many different species to return and thrive. You do this not by planting only certain kinds of plants to the exclusion of the others, but by doing what Joel's saying, or pitting the soil so seeds and mulch and water will find their way to each other."

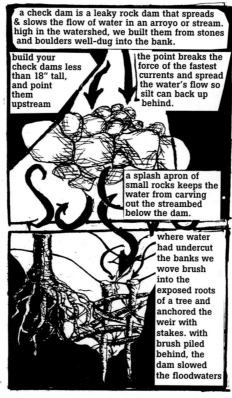

a check dam is a leaky rock dam that spreads & slows the flow of water in an arroyo or stream. high in the watershed, we built them from stones and boulders well-dug into the bank.

build your check dams less than 18" tall, and point them upstream

the point breaks the force of the fastest currents and spread the water's flow so silt can back up behind.

a splash apron of small rocks keeps the water from carving out the streambed below the dam.

where water had undercut the banks we wove brush into the exposed roots of a tree and anchored the weir with stakes. with brush piled behind, the dam slowed the floodwaters

I would hope one could apply the same principle to relationships with people— I went on to say— that you act in a way that gives every person the freedom to develop their fullest potential, trusting that they'll do it in a way that won't fuck somebody else over. Trusting that collectively your people, your neighborhood, your community know a hell of a lot more than any one person. If we work in this way, spreading mulch on sparse livelihoods, creating strategic turbulence in the rush of the mainstream, creating favorable locations for kids to grow up in, and scattering knowledge as free and wide as a dandelion scatters seed, then control doesn't come into it. We're just currents in a very powerful stream.

See Appendix, pages 114-117, for more information on the restoration strategies discussed in this article.

Appendix: practical strategies for sustainable cities

Close to home

solar electricity p. 87

the urban herb spiral p. 103

graywater recycling see p. 95

water catchment see p. 94

keyhole beds p.

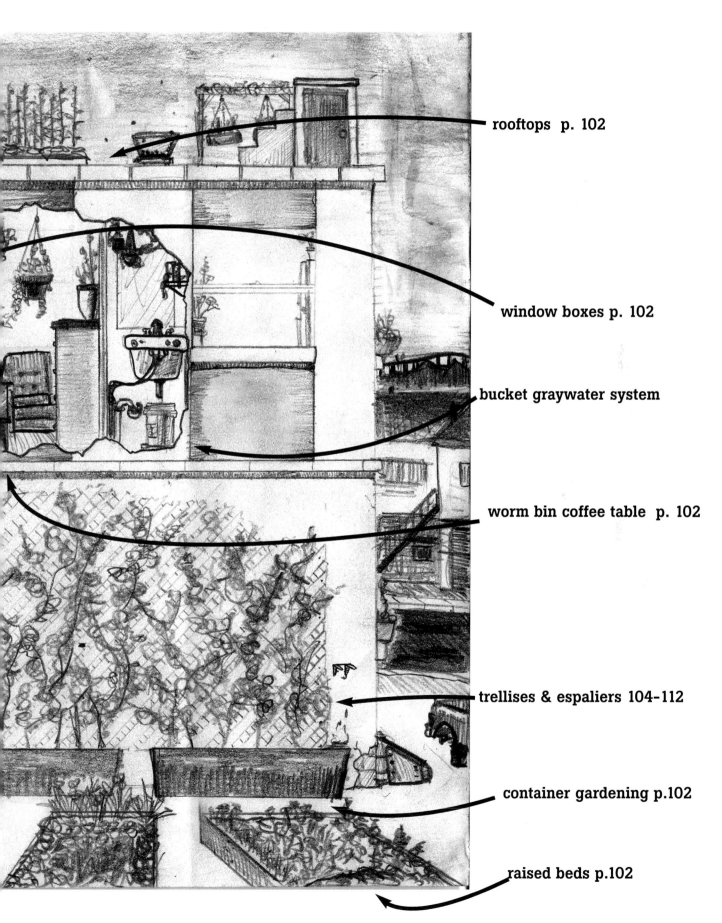

rooftops p. 102

window boxes p. 102

bucket graywater system

worm bin coffee table p. 102

trellises & espaliers 104–112

container gardening p.102

raised beds p.102

Close to home

No space is too small for urban agriculture—even one pot on a windowsill can grow fresh culinary herbs. Urban architecture creates many opportunities for creative use of space, and the urban landscape is full of "trash" waiting to be put to a good use. Gardens on balconies or up against apartment walls are convenient to care for and harvest from—imagine reaching out your second-story window to pick grapes from a trellised vine!

Close to home there are many opportunities to recycle "waste" by recycling graywater and composting food scraps and generate energy with rooftop solar panels. From potatoes growing in shopping carts that get wheeled out onto a 4th-floor balcony during the daytime to worm-bin coffee tables, agricultural opportunies are limited only by the height of your walls and your imagination!

Window boxes, raised beds, containers and rooftops

Most vegetables and herbs—and many fruit trees and berries—can be grown in containers. Almost any container can be used to grow plants, from milk crates lined with plastic to old sinks to wooden packing crates to old shoes. Just make sure you poke some holes in the bottom for drainage. Containers can sit on the ground (patios, porches), on balconies and rooftops or bolt them to windowsills, railings or exterior walls, or hang pots from porch roofs or awnings. Raised beds are containers without bottoms, used on rooftops, and on top of pavement or contaminated soil. If your soil is not polluted and you want your plants to send their roots below the soil, break up the ground underneath with a digging fork or pickaxe. Raised beds can be edged with salvage lumber, railroad ties, rocks, cob or broken concrete. On roofs, use wood or other light material.

Soil mix for raised beds:
7 parts good garden soil, for structure and micronutrients
2 parts compost, for fertility
2 parts sand for drainage
micronutrient mix (see below)

Lightweight soil mix for rooftops and balconies
1 parts styrafoam packaging material (not the biodegradable kind)
2 parts rotted manure or good compost
4 parts city compost
micronutrient mix (see below)
also see other soil mixes under nurseries below.

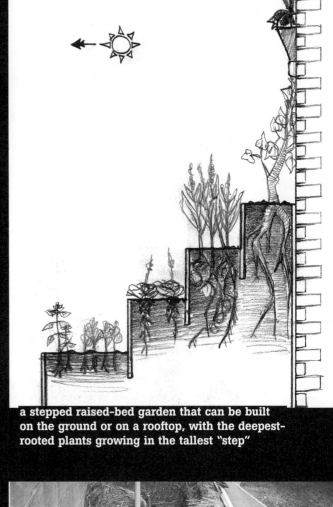

a stepped raised-bed garden that can be built on the ground or on a rooftop, with the deepest-rooted plants growing in the tallest "step"

a cold frame made out of straw bales and recycled windows for starting seeds; this type of cold frame can also be used to protect garden beds from frost

102

This portable garden can be rolled inside when the weather turns cold. Also add a trellis?

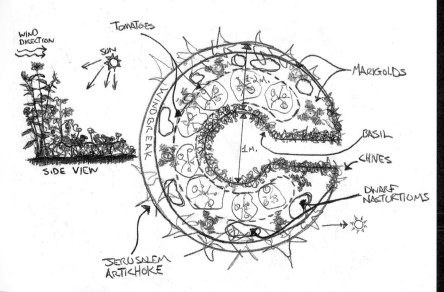

Side view of an herb spiral made out of broken concrete

plan for a keyhole bed & suntrap with common ingredients growing next to each other

Window greenhouses & cold frames

Gardeners in cold climates want some way to start seedlings indoors several weeks before they can plant outside. Guerrilla gardeners in London have this to say: "You can start seeds in a south/east facing window or transform your window into a greenhouse by putting shelves across it. Other improvements could be putting double glazing (clear plastic is enough) or aluminum foil on the side of the shelf, or behind them if you're not bothered about light coming into the room. On a flat roof or sunny patio build a cold frame, a box with a window lid inclined towards the sun."

In very cold climates you can make insulated cold frames out of straw bales and old windows. When you're done with the bales, use them in erosion control projects or as mulch for your garden.

The urban herb spiral

The herb spiral is a popular permaculture concept because it's a simple demonstration of patterning, or modeling garden designs on compact, efficient patterns in nature. You can make your herb spiral out of rocks, but we prefer to use urbanite (a.k.a. broken concrete). The lowest spot could be a miniature pond for growing watercress or lotus; plant the rest of the spiral with the tallest plants on top, keeping in mind which plants like sun or shade.

Keyhole beds

Keyhole beds are modeled on a natural pattern common in urban environments: locked doors and keys. Naw... seriously, keyhole beds save a lot more space than rows or beds with rows in between, and what's this obsession with straightness anyway? In really tight spaces, make your paths and keyholes out of brick or urbanite, as wood chips tend to spread out and take over valuable bed space.

Sun traps

Once you've laid out your paths and keyholes, you can plant your beds to create suntraps, keeping in mind companion planting and how you're gonna harvest. In general, plant tall plants in south facing arcs around the perimeter of the bed, and also where they'll shelter the smaller plants from wind. One possible plant guild is illustrated.

Walls and fences

If you think in terms of vertical space, nearly all urban walls and fences can be transformed into useful growing space. In hot places, vines on walls can replace energy-guzzling air conditioners. On south and west facing walls, vines block the hot afternoon sun, and can be strategically placed to shade west windows, which make many buildings uninhabitably hot. On north-facing walls, dense, woody vines help insulate the building from cold winds. Vines on trellises can be placed to shade windows and walkways, to channel cool breezes or block cold winds, to create private areas and to filter street noise and pollution.

Trellises and espaliers

Trellises are a great way to save space and to add a vertical dimension to your garden. Vertical space gives your garden volume, which makes it much more interesting and productive than a flat space on the ground. Beans and peas will grow up a single string, while grapes and kiwis need strong supports made from wood or metal. Trellises can be made from many scrap materials, including remesh, window bars, metal bed frames and springs and bicycle wheels. You can place your trellis to shade walls, porches and windows, block wind and provide privacy from the noisy, polluted street.

Apples, pears, and stone fruits can be trained (or espaliered) along walls, over arches or close to the ground. New growth on fruit trees is very flexible and easy to train into virtually any shape. First stretch wires tightly a few inches out from a wall. Tie bamboo canes to the wires, and attach the branches tightly to them using flexible plastic nursery tape or other adjustable ties (used bike tube works great). Train new growth each year, pruning off branches that don't work with your design, and loosen ties on older branches. Prune off all branches that grow towards the wall or fence, and prune branches that grow outwards at the first bud to produce fruiting spurs. For more information, check out the pruning books in the resource section.

Solar ovens

Forget fossil fuels—you can cook with the sun! Solar ovens can be made entirely from scrap materials such as plywood, corrugated cardboard and mylar from potato chip bags and balloons! To build the solar oven that is illustrated, we bought nothing mor e than black barbeque paint for the inside of the box, screws, and glue for attaching the reflective material. This oven reaches 350° at noon on a sunny day, and the food tastes delicious!

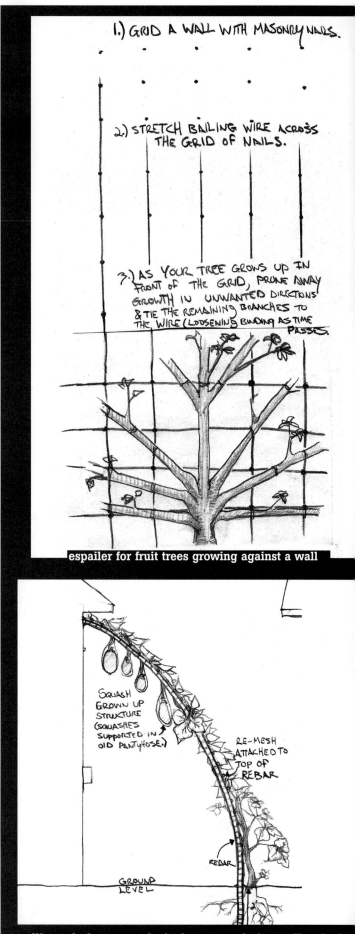

1.) GRID A WALL WITH MASONRY NAILS.

2.) STRETCH BAILING WIRE ACROSS THE GRID OF NAILS.

3.) AS YOUR TREE GROWS UP IN FRONT OF THE GRID, PRUNE AWAY GROWTH IN UNWANTED DIRECTIONS & TIE THE REMAINING BRANCHES TO THE WIRE (LOOSENING BINDING AS TIME PASSES).

espalier for fruit trees growing against a wall

SQUASH GROWN UP STRUCTURE (SQUASHES SUPPORTED IN OLD PANTYHOSE.)

RE-MESH ATTACHED TO TOP OF REBAR

REBAR

GROUND LEVEL

a trellis made from remesh shades a west-facing wall and window & reduces energy use by passively cooling the house

Buried unglazed pots for irrigation

Unglazed pots buried in the ground provide a constant supply of water right to the root zone of plants. narrow-necked *ollas* work well. Plant water-loving plants close to the pots; other plants can be planted up to 18" from the pot. Cover the tops of the pots to reduce evaporation.

This irrigation system works well with graywater-treatment wetlands that deliver small amounts of water at unpredictable times. Just move the hose from one pot to the other as they dry out (4-5 days depending on your pot).

Worm compost

Worm boxes are a great way that even apartment-dwellers can compost their kitchen scraps. With a little care a worm box is clean and odorless and produces worm castings and nutrient rich worm "tea." Any plastic or wooden box can be turned into a worm box as long as it has a spout to drain off the "tea," a lid, and a barrier such as an elevated screen or a few inches of gravel to keep the worms from drowning in the tea at the bottom of the box.

If your worm box is outside, make sure it's out of the sun— if the temperature in the box exceeds 89° F the worms die instantly. Begin by putting a thick layer of shredded newspaper or corrugated cardboard on top of the gravel. Then add some food scraps, a few handfuls of redworms, and another layer of newspaper or cardboard (the worms love the glue in corrugated cardboard). Do this every time you add food scraps, and minimize the amount of meat and grease you put in the bin. You can also keep worms in a shaded, shallow pit in the ground, or in larger outdoor boxes for larger households or entire apartment buildings.

Dilute the worm tea with water and use it as a liquid fertilizer for fruits or veggies. The castings can be harvested after several months and used to make deliciously rich soil.

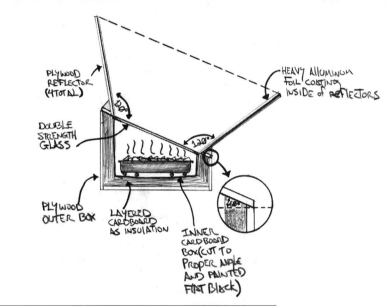

solar oven made in an afternoon from glass, aluminum foil and cardboard in a community garden in Minneapolis

PLYWOOD REFLECTOR (4 TOTAL)

HEAVY ALLUMINUM FOIL COATING INSIDE of REFLECTORS

DOUBLE STRENGTH GLASS

PLYWOOD OUTER BOX

LAYERED CARDBOARD AS INSULATION

INNER CARDBOARD BOX (CUT TO PROPER ANGLE AND PAINTED FLAT BLACK)

plan for an efficient solar oven made from recycled materials. The outer box and reflectors can also be made from cardboard or other heat-safe material.

a passive irrigation system for keyhole beds or other small areas

Community Gardens, Neighborhoods, &the City at Large

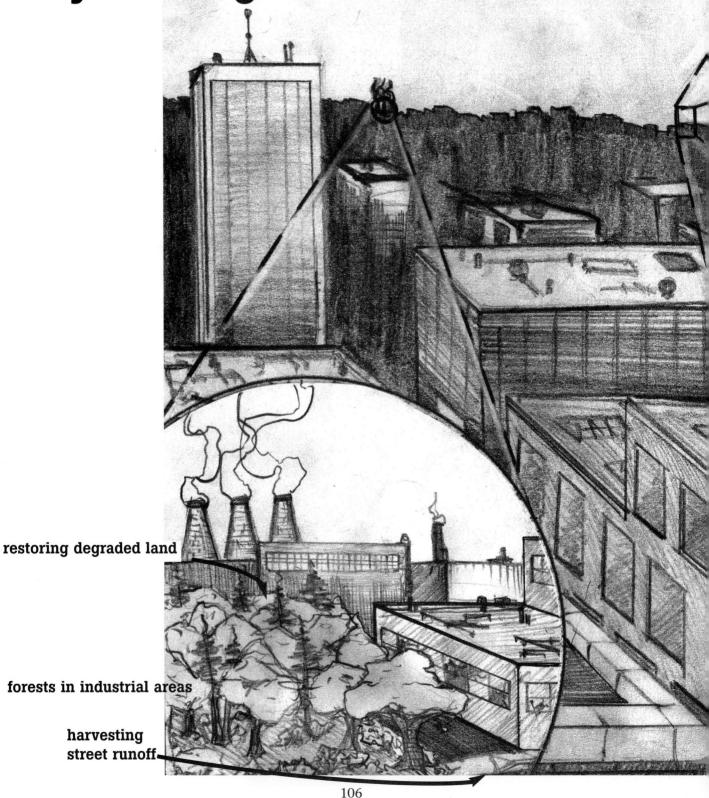

restoring degraded land

forests in industrial areas

harvesting
street runoff

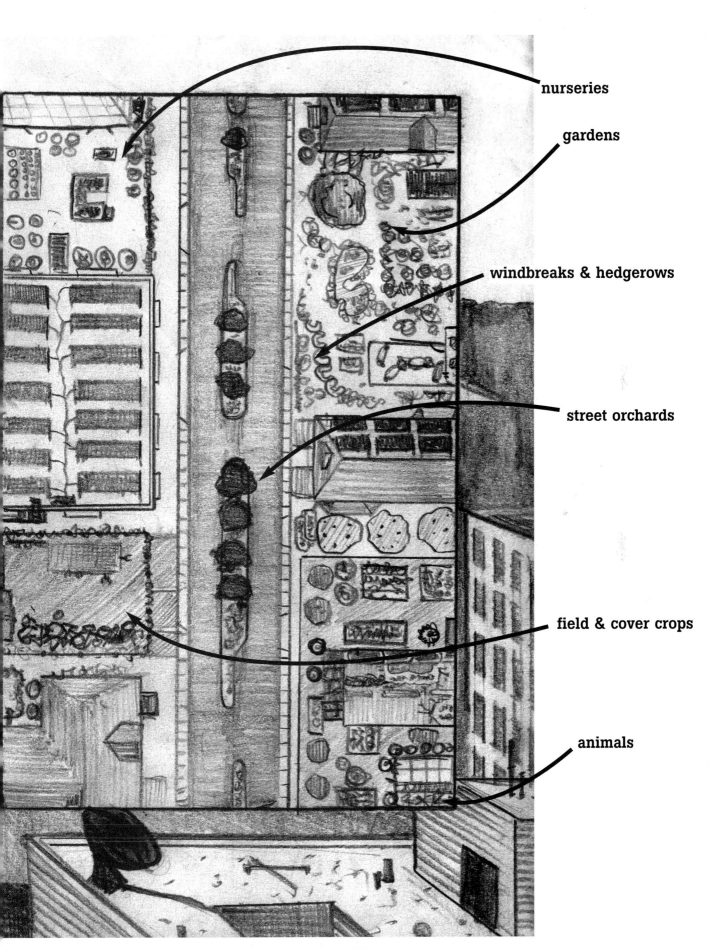

nurseries

gardens

windbreaks & hedgerows

street orchards

field & cover crops

animals

The Block...

Beyond the immediate spaces around our houses, backyards, vacant lots or neighbor's yards give urban gardeners a place to grow some serious food. By using a little ingenuity and the abundant resources of the urban environment, we can turn this land into incredibly productive food forests.

Animals

Farm animals were once common in cities, but have been pushed out by restrictive zoning. However, many animals are useful to us as sources of food, manure, heat, hides and wool, and can be raised much more humanely in an organic garden or urban farm than on factory farms. Integrated into gardens, rabbits and sheep mow lawns, geese weed, pigs and chickens till and fertilize the soil, wild birds plant and disperse seeds, deer and goats prune trees, bees pollinate, and a wide range of insects, birds and bats catch insects that we consider pests. Animals in the garden restore natural cycles that were broken by urbanization. Rather than growing or buying feed for your chickens, let them eat amaranth— a common weed whose seeds contain 14% protein. They can live in movable "tractors" where they till and scratch, eat bugs and fertilize beds between crops. The chicken-heated greenhouse makes use of another important resource: animal's body heat.

Everyone should build structures to attract birds, bats and native pollinators to their garden, and create habitat for other beneficial insects. Even a small pond will probably attract dragonflies, whose larvae eat mosquito larvae. See sidebar for a list of plants for attracting beneficial insects.

Small ponds

Ponds can be used for raising fish and aquatic plants or simply for their beauty and benefit to wildlife. In addition, you can grow many useful medicinal plants in shallow bogs around the edge of ponds. Ponds can hold storm runoff, store treated graywater, or you can fill

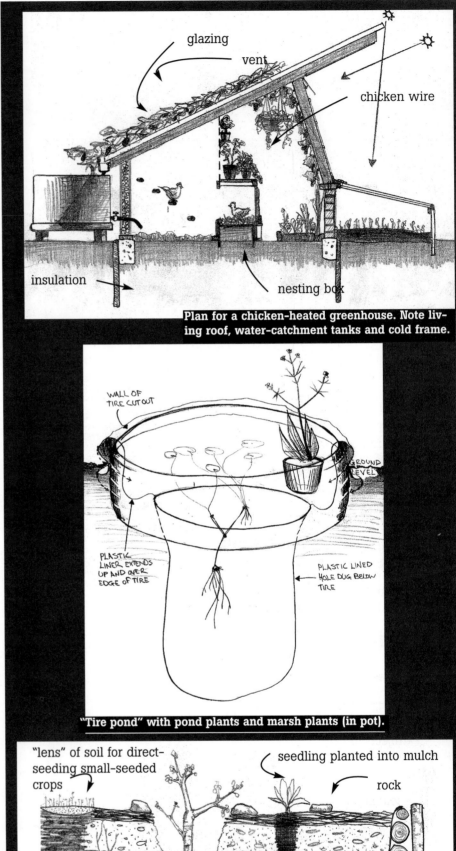

Plan for a chicken-heated greenhouse. Note living roof, water-catchment tanks and cold frame.

"Tire pond" with pond plants and marsh plants (in pot).

sheet mulched bed (bottom to top): cardboard, "coarse mulch" (small branches, cornstalks etc), leaves or straw, and decorative mulch such as cocoa hulls.

108

them with a hose. Use thick rubber pond liner, thick, strong shower curtains, or thin plastic sandwiched between 2 layers of carpet. Ponds can be any size, although shallow ponds may fill up with algae and be too hot for fish. To deter mosquitos, attract dragonflies to your pond (their larvae eat mosquito larvae) or stock your pond with mosquito fish.

Sheet Mulch

You can make an instant garden on top of a lawn or weedy bare soil by sheet mulching. Sheet mulching is the lazy person's way to make soil. Don't expect the same yields as a double-dug garden the first year, but in time the mulch will turn into rich, healthy soil. If you have heavy, clayey soil, sprinkle gypsum on the ground before laying down the mulch. If you are using manure which may contain weed seeds, place it on top of the gypsum. Cover with a layer of cardboard, several sheets of newspaper or old cotton or wool clothes. Make sure there are no places where grass or weeds can come through. Next, add branches, straw, or similar coarse organic material. Then comes a layer of leaves, coffee grounds, small amounts of sawdust— any fine-textured organic material. Top it off with cocoa hulls, wood chips or other nice looking "waste product." The best strategy is to build your mulch beds in the fall, plant a winter cover crop, then plant into the decomposed mulch the following spring. You can also plant your bed the day you make it. Here's how:

For fine seed: make a lens of rich soil 1" deep over rich, fine mulch. The seeds will germinate in the soil, then send their roots into the mulch.

For seedlings: dig a hole in the mulch and throw in a few handfuls of soil. Plant the seedling into the soil.

Trees: plant trees before you sheet mulch, and omit all but the cardboard layer.

Nurseries

A nursery is essential for any urban wilds project. In the shade of other trees, grow vegetable starts, herbs and other botanical curiosities, store donated fruit trees and propagate native plants. Nurseries are great "portable agriculture" projects for those without secure land, and many people make a bit of cash on the side from farmer's market sales.

Standard soil mixes for containers use peat, perlite and vermiculite— all mined, energy-intensive materials— for lightweight water retention and drainage. Locally available, recycled, no-cost alternatives are:

Peat, vermiculite: if you live near old lumber mills, well decomposed sawdust (at least 30 years old) is an excellent inert water-holding material for seedling mixes and container gardening.

Perlite: if weight is not an issue, you can probably find sand closer to home than perlite. For you urban scavengers, try using styrafoam peanuts. Sounds scary, but there are some advantages to the 3000 year half-life of this stuff.

How to get free plants:

Propagation from seeds, cuttings, root division. Seeds can be collected in parks, gardens, alleys, and neighbors yards. Also, seed companies will usually donate "outdated" seed, which is perfectly fine to grow. Cuttings can be taken from anywhere, some plants can be grown from just a single leaf cutting. Root division is a great way to propagate, ask your neighbors what they've got too much of. Many local nurseries throw "distressed" plants in the dumpster... you can get them there or ask the store to save them for you.

Plants are easy to propagate. Anyone making the commitment to regaining control over her food supply must learn how to do it. This does not need to take up very much space and often fulfills the urge to procreate! It reminds me of the old adage, "You can give someone a fish and feed her for a day, or teach her to fish and feed her for a lifetime." Same concept here.

...the Neighborhood...

Beyond our homes and community gardens, the city is full of land that we can use to provide us with food, fuel and building materials. From 6-acre abandoned schoolyards to 60 square foot curb strips, the city is full of vacant land that we can use to grow field crops and orchards. Ideally, we'd plant these where they'd receive some care, however these crops definitely need a lot less attention than tender vegetables.

Food Forests in Parks, Curb Strips and Medians

A tactic for creating street orchards proposed by guerrilla gardeners in Washington, D.C. is to take trees door-to-door in your neighborhood, offering to plant them for anyone who agrees to water and care for them. In one L.A. neighborhood kids pick peaches from the trees around their apartment and sell them to neighbors.

If you don't have city sprinklers to water your trees, you'll have to water them yourself. Two people can haul 30 gallons of water on a skateboard. Or you can divert street runoff to water your trees. (see p. 114)

Grafting apple branches on crabapple trees or wild plums growing in alleys or over fences can have wonderful

Bud Grafting

Budding can be used to propagate woody plants or to add new and possibly different branches to pre-existing trees. For example, you could bud graft a fruiting sweet cherry onto an ornamental cherry blossom tree in a park. Budding is best done in the spring.

one: on a small branch of a tree or on rootstock, cut a one inch vertical slit, and a smaller perpendicular cut, forming a "T" shape.

two: remove the leaves from a small branch of the tree you want to reproduce. leave a little bit of the stem to be used as a handle.

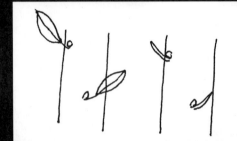

three: cut out the bud. start from below, cutting upward with a sharp knife. cut across the top of the cut you just made and remove the bud. be careful not to touch the cut side of the bud.

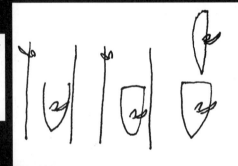

four: insert the bud from the top of the "T" cut until the tops are level.

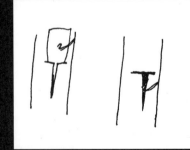

five: wrap up the area around the graft with whatever you've got around: rafia, tape, rubber bands, strips of bike tube. this needs to be fairly snug to keep the graft together and to prevent it from drying out. you can paint the graft area with pruning sealer, roofing tar or something similar to seal the graft.

results. You can graft many branches onto each tree, each with its own variety of fruit.

Here's step by step instructions for planting guerrilla garden fruit trees.

1. You can rent a concrete saw or get out a sledge hammer to remove a portion of the sidewalk (allow enough space for pedestrians to pass).

2. Dig yourself a hole. A garden fork is better than a shovel because it leaves spaces where the roots of the tree can penetrate the surrounding soil. If you use a shovel, rough up the edges of the hole with the edge of the shovel.

3. Take the tree out of its pot or bag. Carefully open up the roots by straightening them out. You want them to spread so the tree can grip the soil in case of a windstorm. Otherwise it will blow over.

4. Place the root mass in the hole and gently cover it with soil. If you want, you can add a small amount of compost. If you add too much compost, the tree will have little initiative to send its roots into the surrounding soil, and that will give it a weak root system. You'll want to cover the roots enough that the "crown" (the place where the roots come together at the base of the trunk) of the tree is at least one inch below the surface. Press the soil down around the tree to form a shallow basin and to get rid of air pockets in the root zone.

5. Add some mulch (straw, wood chips or dry leaves) around the base of the trunk. Mulch holds water and slows evaporation. A thick layer of woodchips will help keep the grass at bay. Leave at least a foot of bare soil on all sides of the trunk— mulching too close to the tree encourages crown rot.

drawings by Loren Hellfire

seed balls in five easy steps:

1. get a bunch of different seeds.

2. get some compost and clay.

3. mix it all together.

4. make it into lots of little seed balls.

5. scatter the seed balls all over.

drawings by Loren Hellfire

Seed Ball Recipe

1 part dry seed mix: 100 different kinds of seeds... choose carefully if you are sowing them anywhere even slightly wild; you don't want to introduce anything that will upset the natural ecosystem. However. I say if you're in a big city, anything goes! Mix up all of the most tenacious edibles you can find and pray for cracks in the concrete as the burdock comes busting through!!

3 parts dry, living compost: Use biodynamic compost if possible. NOT store bought or anything that has been sterilized. The soil fauna must be present.

Mix together the seeds and the compost until its all blended up, then add...

5 parts powdered RED clay: this can be dug when the streams are low, or bought from a local potter.. it must be red clay, which is rich in all the essential nutrients. The more local the source, the better. Mix everything together with your hands until its all a fine powder... the smell will intoxicate you with visions of abundance...

Add **2 parts water**, a little at a time until the whole mixture is the consistency of cookie dough. Mix it with your fingers and knead it until its all together

Now you're ready to start rolling the balls...1/2 inch in diameter is the recommended size; each ball will contain 10-50 seeds.

Toss them on a tarp and let dry at least 24 hours before sowing at a density of at least one seed ball per square foot of land.

6. Water the tree every other day (or when it dries out) until it seems to have established itself. Presto—you've both beautified the neighborhood and provided the public with a source of free food.

Cover crops

Around your street or park orchards, or in your grain fields after the crop's been taken out, grow cover crops to improve the soil. These could be seeded via seedballs, or through more traditional methods.

"Green manures are plants grown to fertilize and create soil the lazy way. Rake the soil surface, removing big rocks and other non- organic material, spread seeds liberally, rake lightly again, water or wait for the rain. Fava or bell beans can be planted in the fall; clover, alfalfa and buckwheat can be planted in the early spring. The ground will slowly start living again, and with a bit of luck plants will reseed and build up earth by themselves over time.

The cheap and easy way to do it is to buy mustard seeds, clover, alfalfa, buckwheat (the kind sold for sprouting), and fava beans from your local market. You can often gather clover or alfalfa a seed from the edges of railroad tracks, other vacant lots and overgrown alleys."

—primal seeds

Field crops

Field crops are grains and legumes— wheat, barley, corn, peas, beans, lentils, soybeans, quinoa or rice, depending on climate— that can possibly be guerrilla planted in abandoned lots. Wheat, rye and oats are grasses, after all, and not 'till you go out with your sickle and harvest them that people realize that you're growing food. Lacking a combine, you'll need

Vertical Space   an international photo essay

Mexico CIty: sidewalk garden and Chayote on trellis to roof

Oakland, CA: Hops growing on a freestanding trellis (foreground) and up a wall, both trellises made from bicycle wheels

Montreal, Quebec: beans growing up string trellis in a patio garden

Boston, MA: Squash on a trellis made from old bed frames

San Jose, CA: Grape vine growing on chainlink fence

Tacoma, WA: Urban fruit orchard with kiwi-covered gazebo

some way to thresh the grain— urban areas should provide many opportunities for a twist on the old "square dance on the threshing floor." Alternatively, place dry bean plants in burlap bags in a driveway and drive over them for a week or so, then winnow the chaff and you're ready to go.Seed Balls

Our work has been profoundly influenced by the work and writings of a Japanese Farmer by the name of Masanobu Fukuoka. He has defied the laws of agriculture and embraced the laws of nature. He makes "seed balls," and uses them for bioremediation and no-till agriculture.

I highly recommend reading Fukuoka and seeing the videos available through the website mentioned in the resources section. There is a little more to his seed ball stuff than I can go into here, and there is a certain point of view that should be understood before attempting to farm in this manner.. .a childlike mind, shall we say?

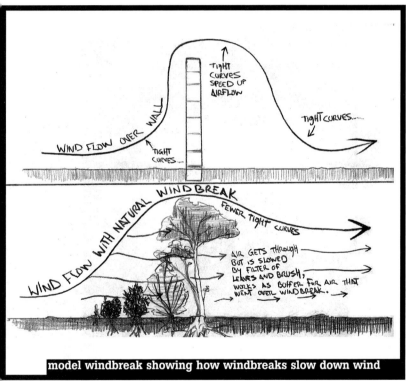

model windbreak showing how windbreaks slow down wind

Hedgerows & windbreaks

In large open areas you may need to grow windbreaks to protect your fields from drying out. A trellis with an annual vine is a quick fix; then plant a mixed, quick-growing forest, possibly with some nitrogen fixing trees. Successful windbreaks mimic the forest's edge: low bushes grow under small trees, with large trees highest of all. A wall is not a windbreak. The goal of windbreaks is to slow down winds, walls accelerate them.

...and the City at Large

There is tons of land on the edges of our neighborhoods and in industrial areas. Unfortunately, many hundreds of acres of this land is contaminated with toxins from heavy industry all the way down to dry cleaners, auto repair shops and photo developing places. Many of these toxic sites are not mapped, because the contamination occurred before dumping was illegal. Some of these contaminated sites (called brownfields) are so toxic from multiple chemical contamination that people can't even live near them, much less grow food. Yet government "clean up" of these sites involves removing tons of soil and shipping it to landfills which are often on Native land or in other poor communities. In addition, non-contaminated land along freeways, railroad tracks, rivers and roads is often planted with ornamentals that have no value to humans or wildlife.

One long-term solution to these problems is to plant permanent forests in contaminated and unused land. Trees have the ability to absorb heavy metals and bind them up in their wood for hundreds of years. Other elements of the forest ecosystem can break down PCBs, VOCs and other toxic byproducts of industrial processes into less harmful substances. In addition, these forests would clean the air, filter storm runoff provide timber for construction and habitat for wild creatures. Imagine living in a city that was more forest than pavement!

In order to establish these forests, we'll need to build soil using compost, mulch, green manures, and animals. We'll also need to stop erosion on steep slopes (above freeways, for instance) and catch water to help our seedlings survive.

Broadscale restoration

In rural areas, grazing, logging, roads and agriculture all cause erosion. Once the topsoil has washed away, plants cannot establish themselves. Without plants covering it, water doesn't infiltrate into the hard-packed soil, so it runs off, causing more erosion. In cites and suburbs, development strips the land of its natural cover, causing massive erosion of creeks and rivers. Eventually, most of the land is paved, and creeks are put in concrete channels or underground. This "solves" the problem of erosion since soil under concrete can no longer wash away. But it also causes flooding and pollution which affect communities downstream, not to mention the effects on plant and animal communities.

In both developed and undeveloped areas, the first step in restoring a watershed is slowing down the water flowing across the land, allowing water to sink into the ground where it allows plant communities to regenerate. Obviously this is easier if you can work on a thousand-acre ranch which covers several watersheds, rather than in a city where the watershed has been broken up into thousands of pieces of property, and the topography has been profoundly altered by city-building. However, there are opportunities to adapt the techniques of broadscale restoration to parks, the land along railroad tracks and freeways, even in streets and parking lots!

The basic idea in restoring degraded land and stopping erosion is to create structures that slow the flow of water over the land and allow it to sink into the soil where plants can use it. On slopes, these are shallow ditches on contour lines, or v-shaped berms (mounds of dirt) called boomerang swales. (See appendix for specifics of swale construction).

A little creativity is all you need to translate these ideas to the heart of the city. In asphalt or concrete-covered areas, remove the pavement from the low spots and plant trees there, or remove the concrete on contour to make swales. In Tucson, Brad Lancaster catches all the water that flows down his street and diverts it to an orchard of date, fig, almond and citrus trees, as well as a lush band of native desert vegetation. First, he busted up his driveway. In its place he made a French drain to drain the street water towards his garden by digging a ditch, then filling it with gravel. Beyond the french drain he dug a large shallow pit to catch and store the water, then planted native shrubs to filter pollutants from the street and to help the water sink into the ground more quickly. From there, the water flows into his orchard, which is planted on a swale to catch the water that falls on the path where the sidewalk would be. (There never was a sidewalk there so Brad made a path that winds through a jungle of cactuses, salt bush, mesquite and palo verde trees.) Large pits or ditches filled with gravel or lava rock can catch and store water from the many gutter downspouts of a city block, and trees planted around them can make use of the water. The only limit to these possibilities is your imagination.

Catching & storing water in the soil

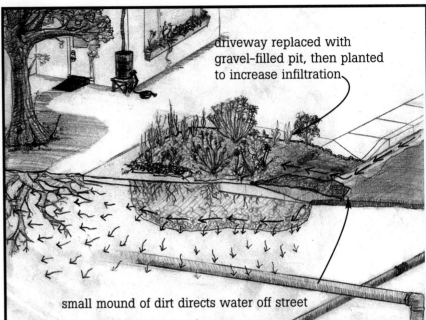

driveway replaced with gravel-filled pit, then planted to increase infiltration.

small mound of dirt directs water off street

Arrows show water flow from the street to the soil at Brad Lancaster's place in Tucson, AZ

On gentle slopes (less than 15 degrees) broad, shallow ditches called swales that follow the contours of the land will hold storm runoff and infiltrate it over time. They will also fill up with silt over time and form terraces. Swales should be mulched to reduce evaporation, and planted with trees.

On slopes steeper than 15 degrees, dig "boomerang" swales. These are v-shaped berms, pointing downhill, that form basins which direct water to one tree. Dig them in a net pattern, starting at the top of a slope (see illustration). The idea is to size them so they don't catch so much runoff that the soil of the berm becomes saturated and bursts. In general, the boomerangs should be larger in flatter areas, and smaller on steep slopes. Soil type will also affect the size of the boomerangs, and how quickly the water they catch sinks into the ground.

Steep slopes can also be terraced with straw bales. Dig a shelf on contour lines for the bales to sit on. Pin each bale into the ground with two stakes (willow, bamboo and rebar all work well). If you can, start each swale or straw-bale from a tree or bush, which will keep water from eroding the ends. Plant a native tree or shrub behind each straw bale. When it rains, the bales soak up water like a sponge and water the trees. The bales will decompose in a few years, and the line of trees you have planted will hold the hillside in place with their roots.

Once the water has reached a stream or arroyo, your object is to spread it out and slow it down. Your work will have the greatest effect high in the watershed, where trickles turn into streams. Here you can build low, leaky check dams out of rocks or brush, or you can use small

an A-frame level is a easy-to-build tool for finding contour lines. Pivot the level across a slope, marking the points where the string bisects the cross piece, then connect the points to find the contour and build straw-bale or earth swales along the contour lines.

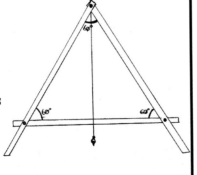

dams called strawbale gabions. As you work, you will become familiar with patterns of water flow. Start small, and watch the effects your structures have.

1. Make sure your dams are "keyed in", that is, make sure they are dug far enough into the banks that the water will not eat around them.

2. Make them broader in the center, where the flow is strongest.

3. Make the dam so water spills over the middle rather than cutting around the sides.

4. Make a splash pad of rocks below the check dam so the force of the water flowing over the dam doesn't carve out the stream bed below the dam.

5. Make your structures no taller than about a foot and a half. Design them so that the silt trapped in one dam reaches up to the bottom of the next.

6. Once your check dams have filled with silt, you can build them up higher.

a series of brush checkdams in a gully near the top of the watershed

Remember that these structures work only in first and second order streams. If your structures blow out, don't be discouraged. Key them in better, or better yet, move higher in the watershed and try again.

My friend Joel says the best thing you can do for a watershed is line up sticks on the contour lines. You can also make micro-catchments on a slope or flat area by pitting the land with a shovel. The pits collect seeds, water, animal droppings and mulch, creating rich, sheltered microclimates for plants to establish. Just laying down mulch on bare spots will conserve enough water to allow many seeds to germinate.

Also keep in mind that the structures you build are only temporary. Their primary function is to allow plants to establish. Long after your swales and check dams have silted up, they'll be visible as lines of trees along the hillsides. These trees' roots reach deep into the soil to hold it in place, tapping into the underground streams and sharing nutrients along webs of mycorrhizal fungi. Their shade and mulch allows other plants to grow, reweaving the web of life that existed there before.

diagram showing where to build erosion-control structures: swales on the gentler slopes at the top and bottom of the hill, straw terraces and boomerang swales on steep slopes, and check dams in small creeks or arroyos.

Where the Wild Things Are

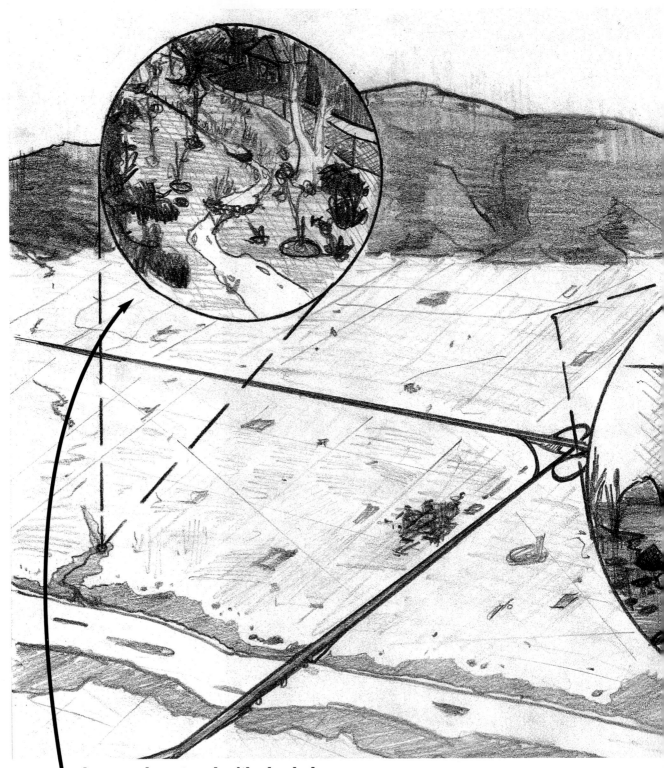

urban creek restored with check dams,
brush piles and native plants

rush pile habitat for small mammals
birds: layer plumbing pipe of various
iameters, large branches & small brush,
onnected to other bushes, hedgerows etc.

Contemporary cities are surrounded in ever-expanding cookie-cutter suburbs that interlock in a dizzying maze of sterile lawns and prefab veneers. Suburbs have a cataclysmic effect on the woods, fields and wetlands that disappear beneath the bulldozer's blade. In people, suburbs cause alienation, for they possess neither the vibrant cultural diversity of cities nor the ecological diversity of wilderness or well-managed farmland. In *A Pattern Language*, an exhaustive survey of livable cities, the authors raise the possibility of cities that are integrated with the countryside, to the benefit of both. They describe "city country fingers" in this way:

> "Keep interlocking fingers of farmland and urban land, even at the center of the metropolis, The urban fingers should never be more than 1 mile wide, while the farmland fingers should never be less than 1 mile wide."

In some smaller cities, greenbelts have kept open space (though usually not farm or wild land) accessible to some city dwellers. And as appreciation for biodiversity and wild places increases, more urban natural areas are being restored. On a political level, creating city country fingers might involve sitting on community redevelopment boards as a voice for the urban wilds, so that industrial land along rivers, for example, can be restored to wild habitat. On a practical level, every community garden and backyard can have areas set aside for wildlife habitat.

A small tire pond or a brush pile provides valuable habitat (food, water or shelter) for wild animals. Bird nesting boxes and orchard mason bee houses will be well appreciated by flying critters. Plants that are native to your area will amaze you with their ability to attract insects and birds, and have the advantage of needing no maintenance once they're established. In addition, many city and county parks contain remnants of native ecosystems, and there is a growing movement to restore some urban public land to its wild state. Track down some of these dedicated volunteers, and you'll learn a lot about plants, habitat and ecological history.

And what about the suburbs? There is a lot of land out there, and suburbia has its own advocates. Much has been written about Village Homes, a suburb in Davis, CA featuring energy-efficient buildings, large areas of common land, orchards utilizing street runoff and productive edible landscaping. Check out *Designing and Maintaining Your Edible Landscape* in the resource section for more ideas on how to bring your suburb to life.

Resources a reading list compiled by contributors

Books & Periodicals
land/struggles/context

Abbott, Jack *In the Belly of the Beast,* Random House, 1981

Alexander, Ishiwaka, Silverstein et. al *A Pattern Language*

St. Barbe Baker, Richard *My Life, My Trees* London, Lutterworth Press, 1970

Berry, Wendell *The Unsettling of America* Sierra Club Books, 1986; *The Gift of Good Land* North Point, 1981

Fukuoka, Masanobu *The One Straw Revolution* Rodale Press, 1978

Giono, Jean *The Man Who Planted Trees* Chelsea Green, 1985

Goad, Jim *The Redneck Manifesto* Simon & Schuster, 1997

Jensen, Derrick *A Language Older Than Words* Context Books, 2000

Lipsitz, George *A Life in the Struggle: Ivory Perry and the Culture of Resistance,* Philadelphia, Temple University Press, 1988

Shakur, Assata *Assata* L. Hill, 1987

Silko, Leslie Marmon *The Almanac of the Dead* New York, Simon & Schuster, 1991

Storl, W. *Culture and Horticulture: a philosophy of gardening* Bio-dynamic Literature, 1979

Tzu, Sun *The Art of War* ed. James Clavell, Dell, 1983

Weisman, Alan *Gaviotas: A Village to Reinvent the World* Chelsea Green, 1998

Plants

Facciola, *Cornucopia II:A Sourcebook of Edible Plants The Vegetable Garden* Vilmorin Andreiux, Ten Speed Press, 1993

Fern, K. *Plants for The Future* Chelsea Green, 2000

Hartmann, H. & Kester, D. *Plant Propagation: Principles and Practices 3rd edition* Prentice Hall, 1979

Nabhan, Gary *Enduring Seeds* North Point, 1989

Permaculture

Mollison, Bill *Permaculture: A Designer's Manual* and *Introduction to Permaculture* Tagari, 1988

Growing food

Kourick, Robert *Designing & Maintaining your Edible Landscape Naturally*

Findhorn Community *The Findhorn Garden* Harper and Row, 1975

Guerra, Michael *The Edible Container Garden* Fireside Books, Simon & Schuster, 2000

Water & Wastewater Treatment

Reisner, Marc *Cadillac Desert: The American West and its Disappearing Water* Penguin, 1986

Van Der Ryn, Sim *The Toilet Papers* Ecological Design Press, 1995

the Guerrilla Graywater Girls *The Guerrilla Graywater Girls Guide to Water,* water/under/ground, 2000

Creating an Oasis with Graywater Oasis Designs, 1998

Jenkins, Joseph *The Humanure Handbook* Chelsea Green, 1999

Publications by Contributors

Living for Change Grace Lee Boggs, University of Minnesota Press, 1998

K. Ruby et. al. *Wise Fool Basics* Wise Fool Puppet Intervention, 1999

Weed Lover by Heather Humus, available from Food Not Lawns, see below for contact info

Seed

Peace Seeds
2385 SE Thompson St.
Corvallis, OR 97333
Send $20 for the latest research journal.

Deep Diversity
Box 15700,
Santa Fe, NM 87506-5700

Farmers Co-op Germplasm Project
30848 Maple Drive
Junction City, OR 97448

Abundant Life Seed Foundation
abundant@olypen.com

Land Trusts

Institute for Community Economics, Inc.
57 School Street
Springfield, MA 01105-1331
www.iceclt.org
Phone: (413) 746-8660
Fax: (413) 746-8862
Email: iceconomic@aol.com

Equity Trust, Inc.
539 Beach Pond Road,
Voluntown, CT 06384.
Tel: (860) 376-6174.

Land Trust Alliance
1331 H Street NW, Suite 400
Washington DC 20005
202-638-4725
lta@lta.org
www.lta.org

Projects

Building Opportunities for Self-Sufficiency (BOSS)
Kathi Kinney
Urban Gardening Institute
2880 Sacramento St.
Berkeley, CA 94702
(510) 843-1307

Cultivating Communities
c/oFriends of P Patch
700 3rd Ave 4th floor
Seattle WA 98104-1848
206.978.6372 or 206.684.0264, x. 3
martha.goodlett@seattle.gov

Detroit Agriclutural Network
Jason Fligger, Urban Agriculture Coordinator
(313) 963-7788

Eco-initiatives
5590 Sherbrooke W.
Montreal, QC H4A 1W3
Canada
tel: (514) 484-0223
fax: (514) 484-3277
ecoini@cam.org

Food Not Lawns/ Weed Lover Distro
165 N. Grand
Eugene, OR 97402
foodnotlawns@yahoo.com
www.foodnotlawns.org

Guadalupe Gardens
Tacoma Catholic Worker
1417 So. G St.
Tacoma, WA 98405
(253) 572-6582

Nuestras Raices
60 Hamilton St.
Holyoke, MA 01040
(413) 535-1789
www.nuestrasraices.org

Primal Seeds Website
www.primalseeds.org

Rooted in Community Network
a network of youth involved in urban gardening
contact Literacy for Environmental Justice
6220 3rd St.
San Francisco, CA 94124
(415) 508-0575
www.lejyouth.org

Free the Land!
The Victory Gardens Project
RFD 1 Box 6025
Athens, ME 04912

to arrange a food distribution in your
area contact:
Herman Bell, 79C0262
Clinton Correctional Facility
PO Box 2001
Dannemora, NY 12929-2001

To contact other gardeners or projects featured in this
book, write to:

the Urban Wilds Project
PO Box 3831
Oakland, CA 9460o

Notes on contributors

Lauraxe lives in Oakland, CA in a house full of people, cats and chickens with a pond, 10-foot-tall cattails, solar panels, a graywater system, a beautiful garden and a pedal-powered washing machine.

Carla Campbell worked as an intern at The Food Project's Pollution Prevention Program in Roxbury, MA, using gardens to address environmental justice issues in her community.

Dan Dorsey, B.S. Forestry, is a permaculture and strawbale house designer in Tucson. He built the first to-code strawbale house in Pima County, AZ in 1991, and lives at Mesquite Tree Permaculture Site, an intensively planted and managed mini farm in Tucson.

Heather Humus is a seed saver and gardener at Food Not Lawns in Eugene, OR. She puts out the "Weed Lover," a zine on permaculture and natural farming.

Sol Kinnis is working with Common Ground community-mapping project and the Lifecycles Project on Vancouver Island. She spent three months in Havana, Cuba working with the Antonio Nuñez Jiménez Foundation for Nature and Humanity, as part of a CIDA internship program, helping to initiate research on backyard and small lot gardening in inner-city Havana for a long-term community mapping project.

Tim Krupnik lives in Davis, CA.

Isabel Moore lives in the Bronx. She started out as an activist, and got involved in gardening when ten gardens in her neighborhood became threatened by bulldozers. Now she loves to garden, thanks to all the wonderful gardeners who are the Bronx United Gardeners.

Andrea del Moral lives in overalls and oscillates between rural farm and philosophy places (Institute for Social Ecology, VT) and urban garden and project places (Oakland, CA). Agriculturally, she prefers the challenge and change of seasons and the untapped resources of the city. She works on the Peralta After-School Garden in Fruitvale and is collaborating on a dance-word performance on water, to be performed in the suburbs. Sometimes she thinks of writing books but may think a few more times after watching cle@ pull this one off.

Tomaz Petauer is an anarchist and urban gardener who lives in Ljubljana, Slovenia.

Ever have the urge to start a guerrilla garden? Contact **John Plantain** at benature@hotmail.com.

K.Ruby is an artist, activist, bodyworker, naturalist, gardener and beekeeper living in Oakland, CA. Best known for her work as co-founder and director of Wise Fool Puppet Intervention and the PuppetLOVE! Festival of Radical Puppetry, she has turned in recent years to her love of plants as an aspiring botanist, permaculturist and pollination ecology geek.

Errol Schweizer was the 1994 pie-eating champion of Bronx House Community Center. Sometime in the mid-90's when comic books got too expensive, he fell head-first into radical politics. He can usually be found doing community organizing on environmental justice, anti-prison and anti-globalization issues.

Sonja Sveisend is a prison activist and Victory Gardens Project volunteer. She lives in Seattle.

Bruce Triggs has lived at the Tacoma Catholic Worker for the past nine years. He recently wrote a letter to the local paper about how the elimination of the estate tax might encourage people to kill their family members to make more money on inheritance. He's interested in a serious romantic relationship and just helped his lesbian best friend have twins.

Joaquin I. Uy studies Traditional Chinese Medicine in Seattle, WA; is a volunteer licensed massage practitioner; and helps organize the local Pinay/oy community through AnakBayan-Seattle. In his sparetime, he grows Chinese medicinal herbs, manages a bike collective, and strives to inform folks about sustainable living practices and anything DIY. His favorite vegetable is bitter melon-(*Momordica charantia)*— empalaya, in Tagalog.

cleo is a cowboy naturalist who teaches San Francisco kids about wetlands and environmental justice. A founding member of the infamous Pollinator crew and the Guerrilla Graywater Girls, cleo hopes to have an urban farm connected to a graywater laundromat and community center someday soon.

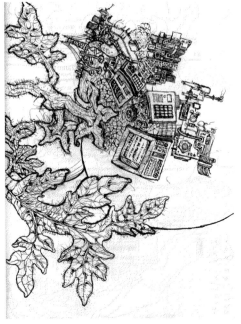

drawing by Greg Jalbert

Index

map showing watersheds in North America